Case
Studies on
Teaching

Case Studies on Teaching

Theodore J. Kowalski
Ball State University

Roy A. Weaver
Ball State University

Kenneth T. Henson
Eastern Kentucky University

Longman
New York & London

Case Studies on Teaching

Longman, 95 Church Street, White Plains, N.Y. 10601

Associated companies:
Longman Group Ltd., London
Longman Cheshire Pty., Melbourne
Longman Paul Pty., Auckland
Copp Clark Pitman, Toronto

Senior editor: Naomi Silverman
Production editor: Carol Harwood
Cover design: Kevin Kall
Production supervisor: Kathleen M. Ryan

Library of Congress Cataloging-in-Publication Data

Kowalski, Theodore J.

  Case studies on teaching/Theodore J. Kowalski, Roy A. Weaver,
Kenneth T. Henson.
    p. cm.
  Bibliography: p.
  Includes index.
  ISBN 0-8013-0233-1
  1. Teaching—Case studies. I. Weaver, Roy A. II. Henson,
Kenneth T. III. Title.
LB1027.K65 1990
371.1—dc19   89-30269
                                        CIP

3 4 5 6 7 8 9 10-MA-95949392

Contents

Preface   *vii*

Introduction   *ix*

CASE 1: Choosing the Right Job   1

CASE 2: The First-year Teacher Is Asked to Do More   6

CASE 3: Drug Abuse Is a Major Problem   10

CASE 4: Departing from the Curriculum—The Results   15

CASE 5: Who Is Responsible for Motivation?   21

CASE 6: Experimenting with New Teaching Methods Leads to
Criticism   28

CASE 7: Asking the Teacher to Evaluate the Principal   33

CASE 8: Questioning in the Classroom   37

CASE 9: Who Goes Where? Organizing Students for Instruction   43

CASE 10: Rodney Misbehaves   51

CASE 11: The Missing Ingredient: Can Excessive Planning Produce
Rigidity?   56

CASE 12: Multicultural Education and the Challenge of Self-image   60

CASE 13: Cheating—A Problem for All   63

CASE 14: Spare the Rod and Spoil the Teacher?   68

CASE 15: From Eagles to Crows—The Impact of Ability Grouping   73

CASE 16: Who Should Evaluate Teachers?   77

CASE 17: Let's Get Tough—Assign More Homework   81

CASE 18: Facing the Decisions Imposed by a Teachers' Strike   85

CASE 19: Building-level Involvement in Curriculum Planning   89

CASE 20: Trying on Teaching Styles   93

CASE 21: The Teacher and Child Abuse   97

CASE 22: Coping with a Negative Faculty   101
CASE 23: The Father with AIDS   106
CASE 24: A Teacher Is Dedicated to Promoting Creativity   109
CASE 25: Why Do We Have to Learn this Stuff?   113
CASE 26: Diagnosing a Reading Problem   118
CASE 27: Covering for a Student's Absence   122
CASE 28: Can I Borrow that Lesson?   127
CASE 29: Dealing with Children's Transition to School   133
CASE 30: The Problems with Packaged Planning   141
CASE 31: Preventing and Controlling Discipline Problems   145
CASE 32: Censorship or Administrative Responsibility?   149
CASE 33: The Challenge of Grading   154
CASE 34: Teacher Effectiveness: Unrealistic Expectations Produce
             Excessive Student Anxiety   160
CASE 35: Gifted Students—Gifted Teacher   165
CASE 36: Introducing New Programs Brings Resistance   170

Preface

Case Studies on Teaching is a unique book designed to infuse reality into the process of preparing teachers. The contents are based on real issues and needs faced by new teachers as they commence their professional careers in elementary and secondary school classrooms. The thirty-six cases offer myriad opportunities for utilizing the case method of instruction. This method has received acclaim in law, medicine, and business curricula. Regardless of the professional context, case studies create interactions that mandate active learning.

Although the foci of the cases are first-year teachers, there are opportunities to examine a range of roles in education. Principals and experienced teachers, for example, are important players in many of the cases. The cases occur in different environments and at various levels of elementary and secondary schools. These cases provide an opportunity to study difficult situations and do not typify the behavior of most school administrators.

We are thankful to our colleagues across the United States who offered encouragement for this book. In particular we express appreciation to the following professors who have agreed to field test the cases in this book.

- Dr. Bob Alley, Wichita State University
- Dr. Jane Applegate, Kent State University
- Dr. Roger Bennett, Bowling Green State University
- Dr. Tom Buttery, University of Alabama
- Dr. Judy Christensen, National College of Education
- Dr. Janet Towslec, Georgia State University
- Dr. Billy Dixon, Southern Illinois University

- Dr. Mary Dupuis, Pennsylvania State University
- Dr. Wilburn Elrod, Indiana State University
- Dr. Jesus Garcia, Indiana University
- Dr. Sharon O'Brian-Garland, Southwest Texas State University
- Dr. Gary Galuzzo, Western Kentucky University
- Dr. Reba Hudson, East Texas State University
- Dr. Don Kachur, Illinois State University
- Dr. Michael Morehead, Emporia State University
- Dr. John Morris, Texas A & M University
- Dr. Robert Morris, Georgia Southern College
- Dr. Gerald Ponder, University of North Texas
- Dr. Tom Savage, California State University-Long Beach
- Dr. Gary Southall, University of Missouri
- Dr. Edwina Vold, Indiana University of Pennsylvania
- Dr. Allen Warner, University of Houston
- Dr. David Weller, University of Georgia
- Dr. Michael Wolf, State University of New York-Plattsburg
- Dr. Bob Wright, New Mexico State University
- Dr. Timothy Young, Central Washington University

Our thanks, too, to the persons who helped with the production of materials. Marilyn Weaver, Diana Meyer, and Jeannine Howard offered technical assistance and advice. Betty Smith, Tamara Peach, and Jennifer Catey helped with the typing. Steve Dickerson, a doctoral student at Ball State University, provided assistance with the research and development of the reading lists. Finally, our appreciation to our students and colleagues who inspired us to pursue this project.

Introduction

BACKGROUND

Case studies are descriptions of a decision or a problem. They are normally written from the perspective of the decision maker involved. Case writers must report the relevant facts of the situation at the time that the problem is being considered or the decision is being made. Once they have been developed, cases are used by students as a way to put themselves in the decision maker's or problem solver's shoes.

In *Case Studies on Teaching* you will be confronted with thirty-six cases that will involve you with the most important experiences that teachers commonly face. Since discipline is recognized as the number-one problem in schools today (Gallup, 1986) and because it perennially emerges as the foremost concern of first-year teachers, some of these cases have been written to help you learn to survive that year (for example, cases on classroom management, discipline, and teacher-parent and teacher-principal relationships). But the goal of this book goes beyond preparing you to cope; this book is designed to help you become an effective and successful teacher. Thus, some cases involve instruction and motivation, and others help students develop positive attitudes toward young people and education. Each of the cases is based on data collected on first-year teachers at Ball State University over a thirty-five-year period—data gathered from teachers working in schools in every geographical part of the country.

As you prepare to teach, *Case Studies on Teaching* should help you in five distinct ways. It should (1) prepare you to identify the major understandings in your discipline, (2) directly involve you in decision making, (3) enhance your ability to think, (4) prepare you to solve problems that occur daily in teaching, and (5) tie together theory and practice.

IDENTIFYING THE MAJOR UNDERSTANDINGS IN YOUR DISCIPLINE

Each discipline has its major understandings (concepts, principles, theorems, or axioms) that must be understood before a general understanding of the discipline itself can be grasped. This has been recognized for decades. In 1932, the National Society for the Study of Education recommended organizing curricula around general principles that "are functional for the individual and enable him [or her] to interpret...experiences of living" (Program for teaching science, 1932). A few years later the Thayer Commission of the Progressive Education Association (1938) also recommended principles as the focal points around which to develop understandings. In the same year, the National Education Association said the following about principles:

> Because they are general, we often meet situations in which they apply. Each application that the child makes of a principle gives it more significance to him. When facts are forgotten, the principle is still significant because it is a functional law in everyday living. (Johnson, 1938, p. 536)

After the launching of *Sputnik I* in 1957, the Woods Hole Conference Committee decided that all American schools should design their curricula around broad content generalizations (Bruner, 1960). In a recent reform report, *A Place Called School*, John Goodlad (1984) recommended that for each subject the curriculum should include a common set of concepts, principles, and skills.

Case studies provide a convenient vehicle for examining such broad content generalizations. As Biddle and Anderson (1986), for example, report "case studies provide an open invitation to generalize."

DIRECT INVOLVEMENT

Only a couple of decades ago the student-teaching assignment was for many aspiring teachers the only exposure to laboratory experience. Furthermore, in many teacher-education programs, student teaching was only an eight-week experience. Today, most students benefit from a full term of student teaching as well as extensive field experiences in foundation courses, introductory courses, and methods courses. Likewise, teacher-education students are benefiting from an increasing number of opportunities in microteaching, that is, they teach brief minilessons to their peers, video-tape these lessons, and critique their own teaching.

These recent yet extensive alterations illustrate a need to provide students with opportunities to observe teaching in real classroom settings. But casual observations will not suffice for preparing one to teach any more than casual observations would suffice in preparing surgeons. Prospective teachers must carefully and critically analyze the incidents that challenge teachers. Furthermore, they must become intellectually, emotionally, and socially involved with the incidents.

Becoming an effective teacher requires more than sitting passively while someone lectures about education. Over fifty years ago, Donham (1931) noted this when he wrote, "The distinguishing characteristic which makes the case system an instrument of great power is that fact that it arouses the interest of the student through its realistic flavor and makes him, under the guidance of an instructor, an active rather than a passive participant in the instruction." The case study method offers you an opportunity to be an active participant. You will engage in formulating alternative responses, weighing the consequences of your behavior, and analyzing the behavior of others.

IMPROVE YOUR THINKING

Becoming an effective teacher requires that you grow as an educated person. That is, you need to develop the ability to weigh individual circumstances by thinking critically and choosing appropriate courses of action. The case study method will provide you an opportunity to learn how to think. As Dewing (1954) explains,

> Human thinking and the human experience are indissolubly bound together.... If we teach people to deal with the new experiences, we teach them to think. In fact, power to deal with the new and power to think are pragmatically the same. (p. 30)

An emphasis of the case study method is on preparing you to think and act judiciously. Although information and experience are valuable, we believe that neither of these by itself can prepare individuals to respond intelligently to new experiences. This supposition is supported by observing the behavior of people who prove the inadequacy of just possessing information by repeatedly acting unwisely.

DEVELOP PROBLEM SOLVING

The case study method has been a major teaching approach in the Harvard Business School for more than sixty years. In fact, it has proven so effective that it was described by a former dean of the college as "one of the major distinguishing characteristics of the educational program of the Harvard Business School" (David, 1954, p. vii). The method has also been widely used in legal education.

We do not suggest that the case method should be used to prepare teachers in the exact same way as it is used to prepare attorneys, but we do submit that the history of case method use in law offers lessons about the use of the case method—lessons from which we can benefit. For example, in teacher education as in law schools, principles should be derived from facts; content should be pursued moving from the concrete to the abstract; and the important principles must be discovered.

Unlike the teaching of law, which seeks to reach "the right decision" (guilty or innocent), the preparation of successful teachers, like the preparation of successful businesspeople, requires developing the skills of identifying a multitude of acceptable, wise decisions. In both programs, teaching by the case method must involve class discussion of possibilities, probabilities, and expedients. Unlike the preparation of attorneys, which seeks to present only relevant facts, the preparation of businesspeople and teachers requires the student to develop the ability to separate the pertinent facts from the less significant and insignificant ones.

TIE TOGETHER THEORY AND PRACTICE

Too often the practitioner is heard saying that "we deal in the real world, not the theoretical world." Actually, to develop the understandings and skills needed to be a good teacher, you must know theory and you must have practical experiences. Either, without the other, is inadequate. Doyle (1985) observed:

> For clinical experiences to be fruitful in developing appropriate knowledge structures, however, beginning teachers must receive descriptive, analytical feedback about performance. In other words, the clinical program must include experience and an opportunity to reflect upon the meaning of the experience. (p. 33)

Participating in student teaching or observing in classroom settings will not, by themselves, lead you to develop better understanding of what teachers do that makes them effective. Koehler (1985) recognized this:

> What is needed, therefore, is much more work on conceptualizing the relationship between teacher preparation and teacher practice.... Students need more clinical feedback by professional teacher educators than they are receiving. (p. 28)

The National Commission on Excellence in Education's report, *A Nation at Risk* (1983), also recognized that this vital link was missing in teacher education. Believing that a full fifth year (beyond the bachelor's degree) is needed to prepare teachers, the Carnegie Commission's Task Force on Teaching as a Profession recommended:

> An approach to instruction that should be incorporated into the design of the post-graduate programs is the case method, well developed in law and business, but almost unknown in teaching instruction. Teaching "cases" illustrating a great variety of teaching problems should be developed as a major focus of instruction. (p. 76)

The case study method as presented in this text will require you to discuss the issues presented in each case and to identify other important issues.

As you progress from case to case you will notice that a general format has been used. You may also notice some slight variations. This is no cause for alarm; at times the nature of the case necessitates these variations. More specifically, the need for variation can be attributed to the fact that in real-life situations very seldom is all the information that teachers need to make wise choices of behavior readily available. Even when this information is available it is often unclear as to which information is indispensable, which information is moderately helpful, and which information is irrelevant to resolving the situation. Thirty-four of the thirty-six cases in this book are based on actual experiences. In each case, slight alterations have been made to disguise the identity of the community, school, and individuals.

REFERENCES

Biddle, B. J., & Anderson, D. S. (1986). Theory, methods, knowledge, and reasearch on teaching. In M. C. Wittrock (Ed.), *Handbook of research in teaching* (3rd ed., (pp. 230–252)). New York: Macmillan.

Bruner, J. S. (1960). *The process of education*. Cambridge, MA: Harvard University Press.

David, D. K. (1954). Foreword. In M. P. McNair (Ed.), *The case method at the Harvard Business School*. New York: McGraw-Hill.

Dewing, A. S. (1954). An introduction to the use of cases. In M. P. McNair (Ed.), *The case method of the Harvard Business School*. New York: McGraw-Hill.

Donham, Wallace B. (1931). Business teaching by the case system. In Cecil E. Fraser (Ed.), *The case method of instruction*. New York: McGraw-Hill.

Doyle, Walter (1985). Recent research on classroom management: Implications for teacher preparation. *Journal of Teacher Education*, 36, 31–35.

Gallup, Alex. (1986). The 18th annual Gallup poll of the public's attitudes toward the public schools. *Phi Delta Kappan*, 68, 43–59.

Goodlad, J. I. (1984). *A place called school*. New York: McGraw-Hill.

Johnson, P. G. (1938). Emphasis of the science program should be based on principles. *National Education Association Proceedings*, 1, 535–537.

Koehler, V. (1985). Research on preservice teacher education. *Journal of Teacher Education*, *36*, 23–30.

National Commission on Excellence in Education. (1983). *A nation at risk: The imperative for educational reform*. Washington, D.C.: U.S. Department of Education.

Program for teaching science. (1932). *31st yearbook of the National Society for the Study of Education, Part I*. Bloomington, IL: Public School Publishing Co.

Progressive Education Association, Commission on Secondary School Curriculum. *Science in general education*. (1938). New York: D. Appleton-Century Co.

Case
Studies on
Teaching

Choosing the Right Job

As Martha Simms completed her senior year at Southwest State, she had only praise for her teacher-education program. She felt comfortable in her content fields, and her methods courses had enabled her to develop a portfolio of materials and methods. In addition to providing techniques and confidence, these courses sparked Martha's enthusiasm for teaching. Although her current term of student teaching was proving to be a rewarding climax to her education, she could hardly wait until it was over so she could get her own classes.

Martha approached this phase of her career as she had attended to its preparation—with intensity and organization. She began by making a list of qualities that she wanted from her school. Then she ranked the qualities and identified those that she considered essential. Her list was as follows.

- be located within a 300-mile radius of her parents' home
- have a majority of teaching assignments in her major field
- have a planning period free from other assignments
- have an opportunity to participate in an academic fair
- have adequate audiovisual facilities
- have a reasonable beginning salary
- have a teacher's aide or student teacher
- be located in a community with an adequate tax base
- be a school where good teachers are appreciated by the parents

After interviewing with several school districts Martha had narrowed her choice to only two schools. Choosing between the two was difficult.

JEFFERSON MIDDLE SCHOOL

The Community

During the early 1950s, Eastside Lakes developed into a plush suburban community bordering a metropolitan area of 300,000 population. As the city continued to expand eastward over the past thirty years, Eastwood Lakes became sandwiched between the inner city and the newer suburbs. Reaching its peak population in the 1950s, Eastside Lakes has since remained at about 10,000. Coal mining is the major industry in the region, and the residents of Eastside Lakes have gradually shifted from white- to blue-collar workers. The once all-white population has gradually become about 50 percent black, 40 percent white, and the remaining residents are mostly recent Asian immigrants.

The School District

Eastside Lakes is one of the smaller districts in the area. Its one high school is fed by one junior high school, Jefferson Middle School, and two elementary schools. The district office houses the elected superintendent, Dr. Jim Grimes; an assistant superintendent, Dr. Max Walker; and three secretaries. A board-room with a long table has the nameplates of Dr. Grimes, Dr. Walker, and six elected board members. Both Dr. Grimes and Dr. Walker are products of the system and each has served in his current position for six years.

The School and School Leadership

Jefferson Middle School is one of the oldest middle schools in the state. The school was developed as a prototype middle school with the expectation that other middle schools with similar innovative characteristics would be developed in the city and throughout the state. Among its most acclaimed features is a media center that takes pride in providing excellent film service to its teachers. It is commonly understood that anything they do not have, they will get. Strong support from a home-based bituminous coal refining industry has enabled teachers to have almost anything they have ever requested, including small classes and planning periods. Jefferson Middle School is fortunate to have Dr. Carole Meadows as its principal. Dr. Meadows has twelve years of leadership experience in middle schools and has spent half of that time at Jefferson. She received her doctorate in curriculum and instruction, and her dissertation was written on the history of the middle school. She understands the importance of involving teachers in curriculum planning.

MARTINVILLE JUNIOR HIGH

The Community

Until recently, Martinville could be described as a sleepy little town surrounded by a prosperous farm community. Because of the relatively high per capita income, the residents place a high value on education. Quality schools are considered a must for the youths of Martinville. Unfortunately, the town's recent growth surge has happened so quickly that motels, restaurants, and schools are in critically short supply. Although the amount of annual revenue generated in the small town's city limits has doubled from $1 million to just over $2 million in just two years, the rapid growth rate has provided no time for planning, and the schools have not seen the benefit from the unanticipated growth.

The School District

Martinville Junior High is located in a town of 20,000 population. Until a rash of factory outlets began moving in just four years ago, the population of Martinville was only 12,000. The junior high school was developed in the late 1940s. At that time, the existing high school building was given up for the junior high students and teachers to occupy, and a new building was built to house the overrun population of high school students caused by school consolidation.

The School and School Leadership

During the past few years, Martinville Junior High's enrollment has grown from 1,500 to 2,800. Mobile homes serve as temporary classrooms for the newer faculty members. The additional growth has provided a broader curriculum with multiple sections of most subjects. Most teachers are permitted to choose between teaching five sections of the same subject or teaching a total of five sections of two subjects; either choice provides a planning period.

Through the years, Martinville teachers have had relatively high salaries. A recently developed career ladder has assured that the school will remain competitive and attract quality teachers.

Martinville's principal, Dr. Jane Wilson, has led the school for the past five years. During this time she has been a strong advocate for her school. This support has been reciprocated by a faculty that appreciates her leadership. Even in a time of rapid growth, Dr. Wilson has continued to encourage her progressive faculty to be innovative.

THE INCIDENT

After interviewing with several school districts, Martha Simms has concluded that Jefferson Middle School and Martinville Junior High have the most to offer. The financial rewards are similar, less than $200 apart. Jefferson wants her answer in two weeks, but Martinville has to know at the end of the week. Both schools have congenial faculties who respect the quality leadership provided by their principals. During the interviews, Martha felt that the Jefferson faculty was a little warmer toward her, yet she had received no strong negative feelings from the Martinville faculty. The decision was not easy.

THE CHALLENGE: You are Martha Simms. Your career is in front of you and your choice will shape your future. Which school will you choose?

KEY ISSUES FOR STUDY:

1. Among Martha's list of desirable school qualities, which of these directly facilitate instruction?
2. Identify any concerns that Martha has expressed for how others feel about her.
3. Compare those qualities listed in item 1 with those listed in item 2. Which are more important as a basis for making a job decision?
4. Martha has limited her job search to a definite geographic area. Under what conditions would such limitations be wise? Unwise?
5. Like Martinville, many schools are experiencing rapid changes in their student population. How should this factor weigh in Martha's decision?
6. Identify some qualities in Martha's list that are missing from these schools. How might Martha compensate for the absence of these qualities?
7. Which of Martha's identified school qualities should she openly discuss during her interview?
8. How should Matha respond to being told that she has only three or four days to accept or reject Martinville's offer?

SUGGESTED READINGS

Bolles, R. N. (1982). *What color is your parachute?* (rev. ed.). Berkeley, CA: Ten Speed Press.

Connell, J. (1986). The work of finding a job. *The Exceptional Parent, 16,* 46–50.

Dunn, C. A. (1985). Actions speak louder than words in job interviews. *Business Education Forum, 40,* 15.

Di Geronimo, J. (1986). The interview game. *Thrust, 16,* 38.

Di Geronimo, J. (1986). Are you ready for a job interview? *Principal*, *65*, 55.

Ginsburg, S. G. (1985). Is the chemistry right? Interview questions to ask—and not ask. *American School and University*, *58*, 11.

Goldstein, W. (1987). Recruiting superior teachers: The interview process. *Phi Delta Kappan*, Fastback, *239*, 1–26.

King, P. E., & Behnke, R. R. (1985). Teaching interviewing skills by electronically mediated simulations. *Journal of Research and Development in Education*, *19*, 44–48.

Ormrod, J. E., & Carter, K. R. (1985). Systematizing the Piagetian clinical interview for classroom use. *Teaching of Psychology*, *12*, 216–219.

Pettus, Theodore. (1981). *One on one: Win the interview, win the job*. New York: Random House.

Sofer, A. (1985, December 6). Job interviews for teachers. *The Times Education Supplement*, pp. 3623–3672.

Travers, P. (1983). Seeking teacher employment. *The Clearing House*, *56*, 275–277.

Vigil, J. I. L. (1985). Ten types of interviewer. *Media in Education and Development*, *18*, 168–170.

The First-year Teacher Is Asked to Do More

Burtonville is a growing suburb outside a major city in the eastern part of the United States. Most residents are commuters, driving thirty to forty miles to work. Only ten years ago, the community was predominantly rural. The rapid development of subdivisions affected every phase of community life in Burtonville, but it had an especially direct impact upon the public school system. In 1972, the school system consisted of two buildings: a junior/senior high school with 430 pupils and an elementary school with 468 pupils. Today the school district has a new high school (1,023 pupils in grades 9–12), a new middle school (878 pupils in grades 6–8), and three elementary schools (K–5 with enrollments totalling 2,003 pupils).

Growth provided untold opportunities for curriculum revision and improvements in facilities and personnel. But the rapid expansion also spawned a number of serious problems. Perhaps the greatest difficulties stemmed from a collision of two distinctively different value systems. The longtime residents of the school district are, for the most part, farmers who possess conservative ideas about education and taxes. The suburbanites, on the other hand, have significantly different beliefs. Newer residents place great importance upon quality school facilities; they demand a broad curriculum with many electives; and they expect a comprehensive extracurricular program. As more subdivisions were created and more houses sold, residents wanting bigger and better education programs eventually gained control of the school board—much to the dismay of longtime residents.

Local property taxes have increased 250 percent in the last fifteen years. Much of this increase has gone to support new school buildings and added programs. The school system recently employed Janice Alton as its chief executive, a former deputy superintendent in the state department of education. Superintendent Alton has embarked upon a vigorous program of employing outstanding teachers. She relates well to three of the school board members (the three representing the newer and more affluent elements in the community); however, she continues to have difficulty with two board members, Edgar Tipton and Byron Fowler, both of whom are farmers and who represent the more rural segments of the school district. The districting plan that governs seats on the school board virtually assures the rural elements in the system two of the five seats on the board of education.

With a growing student population, Dr. Alton has been able to employ twelve new teachers this year. One of them is Bob Kindall, a mathematics teacher who graduated from a well-known liberal arts college in New England. Bob was told before he accepted the position that his teaching load at the middle school would be six classes. Dr. Alton explained that this assignment was necessary because high tax rates and continued growth had combined to restrict spending. Thus, each teacher is expected to do a little extra until the financial situation improves, allowing teaching assignments to be reduced to five periods. Needless to say, veteran teachers are quite unhappy with what they view as excessive teaching loads.

Burtonville Middle School has forty-five-minute periods. Bob's specific teaching assignment includes two sections of sixth-grade math, two sections of seventh-grade math, one section of algebra, and one section of applied math (a remedial-type course). Thus, Bob not only has to teach six periods but he also has four preparations—an especially difficult assignment for a first-year teacher. His classes range in size from thirteen (applied math) to twenty-nine (seventh-grade math).

Mike Simpson, principal of the middle school, told Bob that he would not be expected to take on additional assignments this first year. "I realize, Bob, that you're going to be awfully busy with your teaching," he said. "We don't expect you to sponsor clubs or anything like that this first year." Indeed, Bob discovered that planning four different lessons and teaching between five and six hours a day was more difficult than he imagined, yet he liked Burtonville and thought that his choice of positions was a good one.

In mid-October, Bob received the following note from Mr. Simpson:

Bob,
Please stop by the office after school today. Dr. Alton and I want to talk to you about something important. It shouldn't take too long. Thanks.
Mike Simpson

When Bob arrived promptly at 3:30 P.M., Mr. Simpson and Dr. Alton greeted him. Dr. Alton spoke first: "Bob, we have a favor to ask. We just learned yesterday that Oscar McPhee, our seventh-grade basketball coach, has to have bypass surgery. As you know, Oscar teaches Spanish, and replacing him temporarily will not be easy. Mr. Simpson has located a woman who is willing to accept the teaching assignment, but employing her would leave us with a problem in coaching. I don't need to tell you that the experienced teachers here are just unwilling to take on any additional assignments. My husband graduated from your alma mater, and he tells me you were quite a basketball player in college. You never mentioned that in your interview. You did play basketball in college?" she asked.

"Yes, I did. It was a way of going to that particular school. I could not have afforded the tuition otherwise," Bob responded.

"Well, Bob," Mr. Simpson interjected, "you probably can guess where we are headed with this discussion."

Dr. Alton looked directly at Bob and, motioning with her hand, said, "Before you say anthing else, let me share some information with you. Normally I would not put you in this position. But you know several of our board members have objected to the rapid expansion of programs. They think we don't have the money to pay for all we're doing—and in some respects they are correct. If we can't find someone to take Oscar's coaching assignment, Tipton and Fowler are apt to blow this whole issue out of proportion. They'll get up at the next board meeting and cite this as an example of how we are trying to do too much. That is why I would like for you to coach basketball until Oscar can return to work. That may be two or three months. With your athletic background, you would be acceptable to the community. Mr. Simpson could hire the person he found to teach Spanish. All would be well. You understand, don't you?" she asked.

Bob was stunned. Here he was worrying about how he could get through this year teaching six periods a day, and now he was being asked to take on another major assignment. He also was disturbed by the conclusion that Dr. Alton and Mr. Simpson had reached—that since he played college basketball he obviously had the desire and ability to coach. As he sat there, a number of thoughts ran through his mind. If he said yes, how would that affect his teaching? If he said no, how would it affect his relationship with Mr. Simpson and Dr. Alton?

THE CHALLENGE: Place yourself in Bob's situation. How would you respond to Dr. Alton and Mr. Simpson?

KEY ISSUES FOR STUDY:

1. In what ways does the environment (the community, the school system) affect this situation?
2. What do you perceive to be the benefits and the drawbacks of accepting this additional assignment?
3. Are there questions you would ask before making a commitment? If yes, what are they?

4. Can you think of an alternative solution you could suggest to the principal and superintendent?
5. Do you think you are being treated unfairly? Why or why not?
6. What are the greatest concerns you would have if you accepted this assignment?
7. Is there opportunity for compromise with this situation? Why or why not?
8. From whom could you seek advice on this matter?
9. Prepare a refusal letter related to this request.

SUGGESTED READINGS

Armstrong, D., Henson, K., & Savage, T. (1989). *Education: An introduction* (3rd ed., pp. 188–191). New York: Macmillan.

Bleecher, H. (1985). Why teachers carry out orders. *Education, 105*, 333–336.

Griffin, G. A. (1986). Thinking about teaching. In K. Zumwalt (Ed.), *Improving teaching*, pp. 101–113. Alexandria, VA: Association for Supervision and Curriculum Development.

Hessong, R., & Weeks, T. (1987). *Introduction to education* (pp. 463–470). New York: Macmillan.

Kiff, S. (1986). Combating teacher burnout. *Business Education Forum, 40*(8), 15–18.

Kottkamp, R. B., Provenso, E. F., Jr., & Cohn, M. M. (1986). Stability and change in a profession: Two decades of teacher attitudes. *Phi Delta Kappan, 67*(8), 559–567.

CASE 3

Drug Abuse Is a Major Problem

THE COMMUNITY

Granada is a small rural community in the Southwest United States. A recently developed laser-driven irrigation system has revitalized a community that was once destined to become a ghost town. Yet this boost was not enough to totally offset the damage of the oil slump of the early 1980s. Most of the population are ranchers, including the owners of the two small gas stations and the combination hardware and general merchandise store. Granada's post office is operated by a staff of one, and even he has a small second business that combines a laundromat and a videocassette rental. For a fifty-mile radius the topography is sparsely spotted with oil wells that slowly pump as though to announce the stubborn resistance of a dying community.

A constant flow of illegal immigrant farm workers from Mexico into this community has been a perpetual problem, paralleled by a worse problem—a constant flow of illegal drugs. South of the border, marijuana has become a main crop in the last decade. Its popularity has intensified the long-established drug traffic problem in towns such as Granada, which pepper the southwestern border of the United States.

THE SCHOOL DISTRICT

Because of its vast open spaces, the state has been divided into about a dozen major education service centers. This accounts for Granada Elementary's only obvious link to the outside world. Prior to reorganization, this one-school district was isolated from the rest of the state. To describe the region as remote would be grossly inadequate to most of this nation's citizens who have never dreamed of the vastness of the rural Southwest. Unfortunately, the remoteness of this community is equalled by its poverty. The few dollars that come into the community do not seem to find their way into the schools.

THE SCHOOL AND SCHOOL LEADERSHIP

Granada Elementary is still housed in the 1930s wooden frame building that was built specifically for the school. After a longer period than anyone will admit to remembering, the principal, Mr. Starnes Austin, is finally retiring. A much younger administrator, Mrs. Juanita Quarrels, a graduate of Granada, has accepted the vacant principalship. Like Mr. Austin, she holds a bachelor's degree in elementary education and a master's degree in educational administration, both from the local state teachers' college. Since receiving her master's degree two years ago, she has not pursued further study.

The Granada student body is small and conservative. Like their parents, many of these students are tenacious. They view education as a means to acquire better jobs; and thus, schooling is viewed as a vehicle for socioeconomic mobility. Actually, their concern for social growth is dwarfed by their more compelling desire to earn money. Although during the planting and harvest seasons a few of the parents keep their children home to work in fields, a commonly heard expression is "Go get your education; the crops will be here when you get back." Most of the students apply their family's work ethic to their schoolwork. From their small classes have come many honor-roll high school and college students. Several Granada students have gone on to become petroleum engineers. Others have entered a variety of professions.

THE TEACHER

Jeff Stewart completed his bachelor's degree in elementary education last May with a major in English and a minor in speech. He was a little nervous over his first teaching position, but his nervousness was overshadowed by his enthusiasm. Four years had seemed like eternity to someone who is as active and involved as Jeff. Having finally reached the end of the tunnel, he was eager to get his rewards. The fact that he was given five separate teaching assignments spread over three grade levels (a situation that commonly befalls new teachers in small schools) did not discourage him. And although his students ranged from a section of gifted students to a section of low achievers, Jeff was determined to put his teaching on a personal basis and help all individual students reach their potential. Granada was fortunate to have a new teacher with his level of energy and commitment.

TABLE 3.1 THE TOP DISCIPLINARY PROBLEMS IN 1940 AND 1982

1940	1982
1. Talking	1. Rape
2. Chewing gum	2. Robbery
3. Making noise	3. Assault
4. Running in the halls	4. Burglary
5. Getting out of turn in line	5. Arson
6. Wearing improper clothing	6. Bombings
7. Not putting paper in wastebasket	7. Murder
	8. Suicide
	9. Absenteeism
	10. Vandalism
	11. Extortion
	12. Drug abuse
	13. Alcohol abuse
	14. Gang warfare
	15. Pregnancy
	16. Abortion
	17. Venereal disease

Source: "Blackboard Jungle 1940–1982." © 1985. Harpers Magazine. All rights reserved. Reprinted from the March issue by special permission.

As the end of the first six-week period approached, Jeff's career definitely got off to a good start. His nervous jitters had been replaced by a very busy schedule coupled with a deep concern for "his" students. Jeff's daily conversations focused only on his class activities and upon the youths who were in his classes. More than anything else, Jeff wanted to stimulate students to achieve maximum potential. Jeff's students felt the results of his dedication in their heavy homework assignments, but a few were not making any noticeable progress at all.

Jeff's concern for individual achievement levels was intensified after reading an issue of *Harper's* magazine; there he saw a list of the top discipline problems of the 1940s compared to a list of the top discipline problems of the 1980s. (See Table 3.1.)

One of the students who had captured Jeff's attention was a small, quiet sixth-grader named Julio Martinez. Julio's achievement could most accurately be described as nonexistent. As the first six-week period wound down, Julio had failed all five weekly tests and, in fact, had not come close to passing any of them. He was behind on eight homework assignments. Julio's problems were not limited to academics. In fact, this may have been one of his smallest problems. Julio was a social misfit. Each day when he left the building for recess or physical education his mild-mannered classroom behavior disappeared. He became noticeably aggressive. It was clear that he went out of his way to start fights, often with students who were almost twice his size.

THE INCIDENT

When working hall duty (monitoring student behavior), Jeff overheard a conversation between two students who were discussing Julio. The conversation clearly indicated that Julio was using drugs. Jeff thought, "Sure, this explains his Jekyll-Hyde behavior. But what if they were wrong? Should I confront Julio? What an injustice to falsely accuse a student of drug abuse!"

Jeff considered going to the school counselor, but he was not sure. The only evidence he had was a conversation overheard between two students and Julio's bizarre contrast in behavior. He wondered whether he should just openly offer his help. Jeff also considered asking other teachers whether they had noticed Julio's erratic behavior and whether his performance in his other classes was low. Should he ask these two students why they were so convinced that Julio was on drugs? He wondered, too, what if the suspicion is correct? What could he do? What should he do?

THE CHALLENGE: You are Jeff Stewart. What would you do?

KEY ISSUES FOR STUDY:

1. What additional information does Jeff need?
2. To what other sources could Jeff go for information?
3. Is it ethical to discuss a student with other teachers? With other students?
4. What effects might result if Jeff were to confront Julio?
5. What information do you have that is not relevant to making this decision?
6. What are some other possible causes of erratic behavior?
7. Would it be ethical to ask the two students how they know that Julio is using drugs? What possible consequence might this have?
8. Identify some immediate actions and some long-term actions that Jeff might take to help a drug abuser.
9. Examine Table 3.1. What implications does this information have for future teachers?

SUGGESTED READINGS

Elder, J. P., Stern, R. A., Anderson, Mark, Hovell, M. F., Molgaard, C. A., & Seidman, R. L. (1987). Contingency-based strategies for preventing alcohol, drug, and tobacco use: Missing of unwanted components of adolescent health promotion? *Education and Treatment of Children*, *10*, 33–47.

Gallup, A. M. (1987). The 19th annual Gallup poll of the public's attitudes toward the public schools. *Phi Delta Kappan*, *69*, 17–30.

Goodstadt, M. S. (1987). School-based drug education: What is wrong? *Education Digest, 52,* 44–47.

Johnston, W. J. (Ed.). (1985). *Education on trial.* San Francisco: Institute for Contemporary Studies.

Jones, C. L., & Bell-Bolek, C. S. (1986). Kids and drugs: Why, when and what we can do about it? *Children Today, 15,* 5–10.

Lohrmann, D. K., & Fors, S. W. (1986). Can school-based educational programs really be expected to solve the adolescent drug abuse problem? *Journal of Drug Education, 16*(4), 327–329.

Mayo, B. (1987). A middle level substance abuse education program. *NASSP Bulletin, 71,* 106–109.

Paskert, C. J. (1987). Promoting a national high. *Health Education, 18,* 50–51.

Rodriguez-Andrew, S. (1985). Inhalant abuse: An emerging problem among mexican american adolescents. *Children Today, 14,* 23–25.

Rosenwalk, P. R. (1985). Operating a primary prevention program. *Children Today, 14,* 7–10.

Roasiak, J. (1987). Effective learning demands drug-free schools. *NASSP Bulletin, 71,* 128–133.

Sagor, R. (1987). Seeking peace in the war on drugs. *NASSP Bulletin, 71,* 84–87.

Schwartz, R. H. (1985). Frequent marijuana use in adolescence: What are the signs, stages? *NASSP Bulletin, 69,* 103–108.

Sullivan, A. P., Guglielmo, Robert, & Lilly, Levander (1986). Evaluating prevention and intervention procedures. *Journal of Drug Education, 16*(1), 91–98.

Sullivan, A. P. (Ed.). (1986). Drug use and self-concept (Symposium). *Journal of Drug Education, 15*(3), 73–75.

Thorne, C. R., & De Blassie, R. R. (1985). Adolescent substance abuse. *Adolescence, 20,* 335–347.

Wolford, C., & Swisher, J. D. (1986). Behavior intention as an indicator of drug and alcohol use. *Journal of Drug Education, 16*(4), 305–326.

Wright, L. S. (1985). High school polydrug users and abusers. *Adolescence, 20,* 53–61.

CASE 4

Departing from the Curriculum—The Results

Basil Herman looked forward to the second semester. His first semester had been successful. The three government classes and two history classes—one American history and one world history—had gone well. His first year at Claybourn High School, a larger urban school in a southeastern city, was off to a good start.

He believed the fact he was black was an advantage, as two-thirds of the students in his class shared his culture. He also felt that attending Madison State—a historical black college—better prepared him for working with minority students. After a semester, he was equally convinced of his ability to communicate with the small percentage of white students.

He was buoyed by a recent evaluation conducted by Erving Clements, social studies department chairperson at Claybourn. For the last week he had pulled a copy of the evaluation from his file every day to boost his ego (see Figure 4.1). He even slept with it by his side the day he received it. He pulled it from the file again and stared at it with pride.

"This is one of the finest evaluations I've given a beginning teacher," Mr. Clements had told him.

There were only two areas that Mr. Clements had marked him as "average": confidence and creativity.

"You have tremendous potential," Mr. Clements said. "But you need to start being more decisive. Become more independent. Take more risks."

As he planned for the second semester, he had kept Mr. Clements' remarks in mind. With a new preparation—a sociology class—and three more government classes he wondered how he might be more decisive or risk-taking.

Teacher: __Basil Herman__   Evaluated by: __Clements__
Time: __2nd period__   Class: __History__   Date: __12/15__

5 = superior, 4 = excellent, 3 = average, 2 = poor, 1 = very poor

	5	4	3	2	1
Dress (Appearance)	X				
Promptness	X				
Dependability	X				
Communication	X				
Cooperation	X				
Friendliness	X				
Confidence			X		
Creativity			X		
Judgment		X			
Organization		X			
Knowledge	X				
Adherence to curriculum guide	X				
Use of varied teaching methods		X			
Student interest generated	X				
Classroom control	X				
Grading techniques	X				

Comments:
   One of finest first-year teachers I have observed. Needs to be more independent, creative, thought-provoking, and risk-taking. Should become an outstanding teacher.

Figure 4.1. Claybourn high school teacher evaluation form

The opportunity came during the first day in his sociology classes. Following the curriculum guide he had dusted off fifty-seven copies of Richard Wright's *Black Boy* housed in the social studies storage room and had organized them for distribution in his classroom. After taking attendance in his second-period sociology class, he lectured on the early life of the author, Richard Wright, in Natchez, Mississippi, his move to Memphis and to Chicago. He talked about *Native Son*, how it had marked a high point in black fiction, had been adapted to the Broadway stage by Orson Welles, and had been made into a movie by Wright himself. Throughout the lecture he focused on

Wright's use of characters to describe society. "For the first two weeks of this class," he concluded, "we will look at society through the eyes of Richard Wright in his autobiography, *Black Boy*."

At this point he began distributing the book, handing a stack of the paperbacks to the first person in each row to pass down the row.

"For tomorrow, I would like for you to read the first thirty-six pages," Mr. Herman said. "In the time remaining you can begin the assignment."

Three hands shot in the air.

"Mr. Herman," one student said.

"Yes?" the teacher responded.

"Some of us have already read *Black Boy*," the student said.

"How many of you have already read the book?" Mr. Herman asked.

Nearly one-fourth of the students said they had.

"When did all of you read the book?" Mr. Herman inquired.

"In Mrs. Knoll's English class last semester," a second student said.

"I read it on my own last summer," another student offered.

Confused as to what to do next, Mr. Herman said: "For those of you who have already read *Black Boy*, please reread the assigned pages for tomorrow with the rest of the class. We will discuss the assignment further, tomorrow."

He tried to contact Mrs. Knoll before his fifth-period sociology class, but without success. After talking roll, Mr. Herman asked how many students had already read *Black Boy*. Six students said they had read it in Mrs. Knoll's class during the first semester.

"Bear with me today," Mr. Herman said. "Toward the end of the period I'll talk with each of you who have read the book."

Using the same lecture notes from second period, he taught the class. After giving the assignment, Mr. Herman asked the six students who said they had read the book to visit with him at his desk in the front of the room.

"How was the book used in your English class?" Mr. Herman asked.

"Mrs. Knoll divided the class into five groups. Each group could choose an American writer to read," one student said.

"We chose Richard Wright," another said.

"And you read *Black Boy*?" Mr. Herman asked.

The six students nodded.

"We'll discuss this more tomorrow," Mr. Herman said. "For now, please read the pages assigned."

After school, Mr. Herman rushed to Mrs. Knoll's classroom. As he entered, Mrs. Knoll was erasing the chalkboard.

"Mrs. Knoll, can we talk for a minute?" Mr. Herman asked.

"If you don't mind my tidying the room," she said. "I have a forensics club meeting in here in about twenty minutes."

"I'm Basil Herman," he began.

"The new social studies teacher," Mrs. Knoll interrupted. "How may I help?"

"I'm not sure there is anything you can do now," Mr. Herman responded. "But maybe we can avoid a problem in the future."

"What is the problem?" Mrs. Knoll asked.

"The book *Black Boy* is required reading in the sociology class. It's outlined in the school district's social studies curriculum guide."

"So what does this have to do with me?" Mrs. Knoll asked.

"Several students in my sociology classes read the book in your class," he continued.

"So what's your point?" Mrs. Knoll challenged.

"I'm in an awkward position. I don't know whether to make all my students read *Black Boy* or come up with another assignment for those who have read it. It would be much easier to have all the students reading the same book at the same time," he retorted.

"Mr. Herman, one of my purposes in English is to encourage young people to read. When I give my students a chance to choose what they want to read, I don't get in their way. I want them to enjoy the experience. If that inconveniences you or any other teacher in this school, it's unfortunate. My job's to inspire my students, not make life easier for other teachers," she concluded.

"I don't think you understand," Mr. Herman said. "The curriculum guide...."

"Don't tell me about the curriculum guide. I helped write it a decade ago. Please excuse yourself, Mr. Herman," Mrs. Knoll said. "I must finish preparing for the forensics club."

"Perhaps we could talk about this some other time," Mr. Herman said.

"I don't think so," Mrs. Knoll stressed. "Good day, Mr. Herman."

Mr. Herman returned to his room. On the way back he wondered if he should stop to discuss the matter with Mr. Clements. Remembering the department chairperson's urging to be more self-reliant, he decided not to bother Mr. Clements. "I've relied too much on him already," he thought.

At home that night Mr. Herman developed a list of books written by black authors. It included:

- Richard Wright, *Native Son*
- Jean Toomer, *Cane*
- Ralph Ellison, *Invisible Man*
- James Baldwin, *Go Tell It on the Mountain*
- William Ataway, *Blook on the Forge*
- Ann Petry, *Country Place*
- Nella Larson, *Quicksand*
- Maya Angelou, *I Know Why the Caged Bird Sings*

When he finished, he had a list with thirty-two authors and a book title for each.

The next day he typed the list, made copies of it, and distributed it to his sociology students. He reminded the students that the overriding goal of reading *Black Boy* was to gain insights on American society from Richard Wright's perspective. He went on to point out that other authors' views are as worthy. Accordingly, he told them that they could continue reading *Black Boy* or could purchase or get a library copy of one of the other books on the list he handed out. For half of the period, Mr. Herman introduced sociological concepts that would be covered as they read *Black Boy* or another book of choice. For the remainder of the class, he released students, two at a time, to go to the library to check out a book from the list.

By the end of the week, every student in his sociology class had obtained a book. While most had kept the school copy of *Black Boy*, nearly one-third of the students in both classes selected a book from the list. Mr. Herman was pleased with the resulting interest and discussion. He felt that students' providing examples from a variety of books to illustrate the sociological concepts broadened their knowledge and enriched the quality of discussion.

On Monday morning when he checked his mail before the start of school, he was struck by a note from Mr. Clements. It said simply: "See me immediately!"

He put the note and other mail in his briefcase and walked to Mr. Clements' room. When he entered, Mr. Clements was seated at his desk.

"You wanted to see me?" Mr. Herman asked.

"Yes, Come here and sit down."

Mr. Herman walked to the front of the room and took a seat.

"What is the chaos in your sociology classes?" Mr. Clements asked.

"Chaos?" Mr. Herman countered. "I don't see it that way."

Let me put it another way," Mr. Clements said. "What book is *required* reading of *all* students in sociology?"

"But..."

"But what?" Mr. Clements interrupted angrily. "*Black Boy* is specified in the district's curriculum guide. How can you defend what you are doing?"

THE CHALLENGE: You are Mr. Herman. How will you defend your decision to use texts other than the one specified in the curriculum guide?

KEY ISSUES FOR STUDY:

1. What reasons would you give for allowing students to choose what they want to read in the sociology classes?
2. What evidence in the case led you to give these reasons?
3. How would you interpret the contradiction between Mr. Herman being encouraged to be more creative and confident and the criticism from Mr. Clements when Mr. Herman acts more creative and confident?

4. If Mr. Clements insists that you comply literally with the curriculum guide, how will you proceed?
5. What additional information would you like in order to respond?
6. What information in this case is irrelevant for responding to Mr. Clements?

SUGGESTED READINGS

Carrier, C. (1984). Do learners make good choices? *Instructional Innovator, 29(2)*, 15–17.

Duke, L. R. (1986). Teaching the accepted methods of your profession: The teacher as risk taker. *English Journal, 75*(5), 53–55.

Glenn, C. (1987). Textbook controversies: A disaster for public schools? *Phi Delta Kappan, 68*(6), 451–455.

Harris, I. B. (1986). Communicating the character of deliberation. *Journal of Curriculum Studies, 18*(2), 15–32.

Lehr, R. (1985). Academic freedom: A guide to major court cases. *English Journal, 74*(1), 42–44.

Kamhi, M. (1981). Censorship vs. selection—choosing the books our children should read. *Educational Leadership, 39*(3), 211–215.

Parker, W. C. (1984). Developing teachers' decision-making. *Journal of Experimental Education, 52*, 220–226.

Phipps, N. J. (1984). Autonomy or uniformity? *Phi Delta Kappan, 65*(6), 416–418.

Pratton, J., & Hales, L. W. (1986). The effects of active participation on student learning. *Journal of Educational Research, 79*, 210–215.

CASE 5

Who Is Responsible for Motivation?

Martha and Kurt Grey were finishing a typically late dinner during harvest season when the phone rang. Mrs. Grey looked at her husband. "Who would that be so late?"

"Don't know," he answered.

Mrs. Grey walked to the phone in the living room, picked it up, and answered it to hear, "This is Virginia DeValle, Michael's English teacher. I'm sorry to call so late, but...."

"Is Michael in trouble?" Mrs. Grey interrupted, her voice quavering. She dreaded these calls, knowing how angry her husband got whenever there was trouble with Michael at school. He was a firm disciplinarian who always warned Michael that "the paddling you get at home will be twice as bad as the one you get at school." And he enforced his warning.

"No," the voice on the line continued, "but I thought we might meet to talk about Michael's progress in some of his classes before he gets too far behind. He is having some difficulty with English and math, but is doing good work in other subjects. And he excels in Mr. Graham's agribusiness class. Ms. Martin—Michael's math teacher—Mr. Graham, and I would like to meet with you and Mr. Grey and Michael tomorrow after school, if that would be convenient."

"Well," Mrs. Grey hesitated. "I suppose I could come in. But there's no way my husband can leave the field unless it rains bad. The weather's supposed to be good, so it'd just be me."

"We would really like to be able to meet with both of you *with* Michael, if that would be possible some other time," Mrs. DeValle replied.

"Not during harvesting," Mrs. Grey insisted. "I can meet with you, but

Michael has to get right home to help his father. They can't be there." Mrs. Grey knew that even if a thunderstorm flooded the fields, making them untillable, getting Kurt to school for any reason was nearly as improbable as getting him to church on Sunday. She had been successful at that only once in the twenty-seven years of their marriage. That was to attend her sister's wedding, and not without some struggle.

"I do believe it is important that we talk about Michael's progress as soon as possible," Mrs. DeValle stressed. "Let's go ahead and meet at 3:15 tomorrow. I'll be in the lobby in the front entrance to the school. See you there?"

"Yes, I'll be there," Mrs. Grey responded reluctantly. Having attended similar meetings in the past, she doubted that one more meeting would have any effect on Michael's school performance.

"Goodbye, Mrs. Grey. I'll see you tomorrow," Mrs. DeValle said.

"Goodbye, Mrs. DeValle," Mrs. Grey responded, slowly lowering the receiver.

By this time, Mr. Grey was standing in the doorway between the kitchen and the living room. Having overheard part of the conversation, he remarked: "Michael's in trouble again. Right?"

"No, Kurt, he's not," Mrs. Grey interjected. "Michael's doing really well in agribusiness. He needs some help in English and math, but he's *not* in trouble."

"Michael's going to be a good farmer someday. If crops keep bringing in good money in the next few years, maybe we can buy a couple hundred more acres so he'd have some land of his own, besides helping me," Kurt dreamed aloud. "It's in the genes. My dad and me was never much good in school, specially in English and math," he said, as he walked toward the porch. "I'm going to read the sports."

Mrs. Grey walked up the stairs to Michael's room and knocked on the door.

"Come in," Michael called out.

"Michael, Mrs. DeValle called."

"Oh yeah, what did she want?"

"Don't you know?" Mrs. Grey retorted impatiently.

"No."

"She wants to meet tomorrow to talk about your progress in English and math. She said you're not doing very well in those subjects."

"I'm doing okay."

"Then why do I have to meet with your teachers tomorrow after school?" Mrs. Grey challenged.

"I don't know," he shrugged.

"Michael, I just want to help. Tell me what's wrong. Why are you having trouble in English and math?"

"Mrs. DeValle and Ms. Martin don't like me," Michael explained.

"Michael, you always use that excuse," Mrs. Grey responded angrily. "Anytime you have a problem in school it's someone else's problem. Not yours."

Mrs. Grey left the room, frustrated.

The next afternoon at three, Mrs. Grey arrived at Chester Junior/Senior High School. The Chester school serves the town of Chester (population 5,300) and several small "blinker light" communities—Shire (327), Mulligan (673), Isle City (876), and Avon (464). The small communities are located nearly equidistant from Chester and, as a result, have not operated as independent school districts for more than a half century. Farming and agribusinesses provide most work for members of the communities. A small number of retail stores, service industries, and professional offices, primarily located in Chester, serve the farming communities.

"Good afternoon, Mrs. Grey," Mrs. DeValle greeted, as Mrs. Grey entered the lobby of the school.

"Hello."

"We're going to go to the guidance counselors' conference room. Ms. Martin and Mr. Graham are waiting for us," Mrs. DeValle instructed.

Mrs. DeValle, a sixteen-year veteran at the Chester school, is a mainstay in both the school and the community. Born in Mulligan, her only years away from the community were the four she spent in a small liberal arts college forty-three miles south of her birthplace. Childless, she had "adopted" all her students, carefully charting their progress once they left Chester and "mothering" them while they were there.

She had taken a special interest in Michael, for she felt he had much more potential than he showed. Challenges, such as Michael, spark Mrs. DeValle's interest in teaching. "There have been many other Michaels in sixteen years," she had thought. She had reviewed his grades, talked to elementary teachers, and had initiated the meeting. To some parents and faculty her "mothering" was interpreted as meddling.

As Mrs. DeValle led Mrs. Grey down the front corridor of the building, she engaged Mrs. Grey in conversation.

"The Greys have been in Farmingham County for some time, haven't they?"

"Nearly a century. Both Kurt's father and his father owned land in the county," Mrs. Grey remarked warmly, "We moved into the original farm house when we were married twenty-seven years ago."

"Must be a lot of pride in your home," Mrs. DeValle added.

"Yes, the Greys have worked hard to improve the land—make it more productive. And we've expanded the old farm house. Remodeled the old porch. Enclosed it with glass and put in a woodburning stove so we can use it in the winter. Also redid the kitchen and built on a family room."

"Here we are," Mrs. DeValle interrupted, as she opened the door to the guidance counselor's conference room.

As the two entered, Mr. Graham and Ms. Martin stood. Mr. Graham extended his arm to shake hands, saying: "Hello, Mrs. Grey, I'm Mr. Graham—Michael's agribusiness teacher."

Mr. Graham had come to Chester Junior–Senior High School a year ago, having taught three years in a high school in a neighboring state. At thirty-one years of age he was comparatively old for having taught for four years. After graduating from a major agricultural university, he had tried to make a living as a farmer. He turned to teaching the next year, seeing that he could not support his wife and two daughters from farming alone. With the income earned as a teacher he was able to continue farming on a small scale.

Mr. Graham shares his knowledge and love of farming in his classroom and laboratory. He thinks of himself as a "hands on" teacher, inspiring his students to apply what they learn through projects. He is viewed by students as a popular teacher.

To Mr. Graham, Michael is one of the best students in his class. He sees himself in Michael—a farm boy who yearns to spend the rest of his life on the family farm. He sees nothing wrong with such a dream and is committed to preparing his students to attain it.

As Mrs. Grey shook hands with Mr. Graham, Ms. Martin introduced herself as Michael's math teacher.

As a first-year teacher, Ms. Martin was pleased to be hired in the state where she had spent her entire life. Being close to family had been a motivating force in her choice of a teaching position. She recognized that majoring in mathematics had expanded the choice of schools. As a math major, she had excelled in mathematics throughout her education. She had trouble understanding why her students were not as excited or interested in math.

Michael is a special frustration. "If he didn't understand the problem," she had thought, "I would not be so upset." Not turning in homework or showing disinterest especially angered her. She had discussed Michael with other teachers and had tried, unsuccessfully, to influence his behavior in more positive ways.

"Please sit down," Mrs. DeValle requested. Then she came to the business at hand.

"Mrs. Grey, what we would like to do is to share some of our concerns about Michael's work in school, beginning with Ms. Martin and then me. Then we'd like to discuss some things that we can all do to help Michael. I've asked Mr. Graham to be here, mainly because Michael does extremely well in the agriculture course. He might be able to share some ideas to help us. Is that all right as an agenda?"

"That's fine," Mrs. Grey acknowledged.

Ms. Martin began. "Mrs. Grey, I've checked Michael's prior work in math. He has remained at grade level or better on standardized math tests over the years. As I grade his papers, I believe he understands most of the basic concepts and operations on the surface. But he gets careless when he applies a concept or operation to solving a problem.

"For example," she went on, pulling paper from a stack in front of her, "here are four problems on the first page of this test that are wrong. In all four problems he followed the process correctly, but the answers are wrong. And here are several similar homework papers. It's not that Michael does not understand. He doesn't seem to concentrate as much as he should when he does work in class."

"Is there anything you could share with us, Mrs. Grey, that would help Ms. Martin better understand why Michael has trouble concentrating on his math work?" Mrs. DeValle asked.

"No, not really. At home he gets done what he sets out to do. If he likes doing something and wants to finish it, he gets it done fast and does a good job," Mrs. Grey responded.

"Michael has similar problems in my English class," said Mrs. DeValle. "And about once a week he misses a homework assignment. Ms. Martin says she has the same problem. Does Michael do homework at home?"

"Not very often, I don't think. My husband and I have told him he has to get his work done in study hall. He's got so many chores. And now with harvesting, it's worse. He has to work on the farm from the time he gets home from school until dark, and sometimes till about two or three in the morning," Mrs. Grey noted.

"What about weekends?" Ms. Martin queried.

"Michael and I go to church on Sunday morning. When we get home, we have a big dinner. Then most times, this time of year, Michael helps his father mend fences, tend to cattle, or work in the fields. There's always something to do on the farm, even on weekends," Mrs. Grey explained.

"Michael performs above average in my class," Mr. Graham offered. "In fact, he's one of the best students I've had in a couple of years. What surprises me is that when I give assignments where he must deal with math or English, he has no difficulty."

"Yesterday, the class computed crop yields for corn, oats, and soybeans, based on different weather factors—days of sunshine, amount of rain, level of humidity, daily temperatures, and so forth." Mr. Graham continued. "Each student had his own set of factors and a formula to use. Michael breezed through the assignment."

"I told you he can do what he sets his mind to do and enjoys doing," Mrs. Grey interrupted.

"Last week, students handed in 500-word reports on tracking farm produce from planting to the table. Again, Michael turned in an excellent paper. He submitted a paper on the coffee bean, and traced its route from Latin America and other parts of the world to coffee cups in American homes," Mr. Graham expounded.

"Was the paper grammatically sound?" Mrs. DeValle asked.

"The paper was well-organized. Spelling and punctuation were good," Mr. Graham replied. "I'd be happy to share the paper with you," he concluded, staring at Mrs. DeValle. This was not the first time Mr. Graham felt that Mrs. DeValle was questioning the rigor of his course. Because his course was an elective, most often taken by students on a noncollege preparation track, the class and the student enrolled had often been the object of jokes made by teachers who teach required subjects. He had suspected that Mrs. DeValle had been an instigator of the joking on several occasions.

"I told you Michael can do it. He can do it when he wants to, and if his schoolwork is made interesting," Mrs. Grey added, more assuredly than before.

"Well, we need to work together to help Michael be as successful in all his schoolwork as he is in Mr. Graham's class. I think we share in the responsibility," Mrs. DeValle said.

"We're all in this together," Mr. Graham replied approvingly.

THE CHALLENGE: What can be done to help Michael be more successful in school?

KEY ISSUES FOR STUDY:

1. If you were Mr. Graham, what immediate steps would you take in your class with Michael to provide motivation for him to improve in math and English?
2. If you were Ms. Martin, what might you plan to do in math to help Michael improve in that subject?
3. If you were Mrs. DeValle, what would you do to motivate Michael to be more successful in English?
4. If you were any one of the teachers, what might you recommend that Mr. and Mrs. Grey do to increase your role in motivating Michael to do better in all of his school subjects?
5. Consider alternative consequences of any of the actions you recommend to items 1–4.
6. Describe additional information needed to make recommendations for helping Michael improve in school.
7. Identify information that is not relevant to making recommendations in this case.
8. Is there any conflict between the school's goals for Michael and his parents' goals for him?

SUGGESTED READINGS

Bey, T. (1986). CPR: Helping teachers achieve success with underachievers. *NASSP Bulletin, 70,* 91–92.

Carroll, J. (1985). Detouring students from academic self-destruction. *NASSP Bulletin, 69,* 99–101.

Cattermole, J., & Robinson, N. (1985). Effective home/school communication—from the parents' perspective. *Phi Delta Kappan, 67*, 48–50.

De Bettencourt, L.(1987). How to develop parent reltionships. *Teaching Exceptional Children, 19*, 26–27.

Fairchild, T. (1987). The daily report card. *Teaching Exceptional Children, 19*(2), 72–73.

Fenwick, J. (1987). Middle schoolers: Meeting the social needs. *Principal, 66*, 43–46.

Flynn, F. (1986). Communication time builds a relationship. *NASSP Bulletin, 70*, 97–98.

Fredericks, A. (1984). You've also got to motivate parents. *Early Years, 15*, 22.

Graebner, J., & Dobbs, S. (1984). A team approach to problem solving in the classroom. *Phi Delta Kappan, 66*, 138–141.

Grossnickle, D. (1986). Motivating the motivators: Inspiring the drive for promoting student achievement and success. *Middle School Journal, 17*, 8–9.

Henniger, M. (1987). Parental rights and responsibilities in the educational process. *Clearing House, 60*, 226–229.

Hutslar, S., Litcher, J., & Knight, J. (1985). What motivates students to learn: Identifying the key factors. *NASSP Bulletin, 69*(484), 94–97.

Johnston, M., & Slotnik, J. (1985). Parent participation in the schools: Are the benefits worth the burdens? *Phi Delta Kappan, 66*(6), 430–433.

Raffini, J. P. (1986). Student apathy: A motivational dilemma. *Educational Leadership, 44*(1), 53–55.

CASE 6

Experimenting with New Teaching Methods Leads to Criticism

Unlike State University, which evolved first from a normal school to become a teachers' college with a superb K–12 laboratory school on its campus, a university where teacher education dominated the other colleges and departments with its size, prestige, and teacher-education mission, Comprehensive University has another first mission—research. At Comprehensive University, teacher education is one of a dozen colleges, and its level of prestige does not begin to rival that of the Colleges of Engineering, Medicine, or Architecture, or the Departments of Mathematics, Chemistry, or Physics.

GETTING A STUDENT TEACHING ASSIGNMENT

As an undergraduate student at Comprehensive University, David Brown knew and cared very little about the university's mission. His only concern was to become the best biology teacher in the state. Having grown up in a rural setting and having attended a small rural high school that had only about two hundred students in seventh through twelfth grades, David was relieved to learn that the university's policy permitted students to student-teach in distant rural communities. Because out-of-town placements require additional travel time for faculty members to supervise these assignments, any student who requests such a placement is responsible for persuading a professor to volunteer to perform the supervisory responsibilities.

David thought that he should be granted permission to teach in the high school from which he graduated because that was precisely the type of school in which he hoped to work. In fact, he had dreams of getting a position at his old alma mater when he completed his teacher-education program.

David was a little bewildered to learn that his advisor, who supervised all of the science teachers, did not share his enthusiasm over David's choice of schools. It wasn't the school that bothered his advisor; rather, it was the fact the school was located almost two hundred miles from Comprehensive University. The science advisor, Dr. Ahrens, was already having difficulty finding the time he needed to conduct research and publish the results. Under the university's new policy, failure to produce research, grants, and publications resulted in a loss in merit pay and delayed promotions. Because Dr. Ahrens was an associate professor, and some of his younger colleagues had attained full-professor status, he was becoming more sensitive to the issue.

Unaware that Dr. Ahrens was facing this embarrassing situation, David felt a degree of success when Dr. Ahrens reluctantly agreed to supervise him in his hometown school.

THE STUDENT-TEACHING EXPERIENCE

When David arrived at his old high school, he was welcomed with open arms by the faculty, administration, and students. The school's remote location made the task of recruiting good teachers difficult. He had just arrived, and already the principal was planning a slot for him on the faculty, with full expectation that following graduation David would return to teach biology. Having a student teacher was a new experience for the students in this school.

But no one was more excited than David. His enthusiasm was reflected in his lessons. On his first biweekly visit to supervise David, Dr. Ahrens saw a performance unlike anything he had witnessed in his fifteen years of supervising student teachers. The lesson topic focused on trees. David had gotten up at daybreak and gone into a wooded area to collect leaves. But what Dr. Ahrens saw was much more than a leaf collection. David had brought tree limbs—dozens of them—and the classroom looked like an aboretum.

THE LESSON

Dr. Ahrens entered through the door at the back of the room and quietly sat down. As usual, he prepared to take notes and complete an assessment form, but he quickly became so surprised by David's activities that he forgot to complete the form. David was running from one part of the room, to another, and then another, taking limbs and small trees with leaves and giving them to students to examine. First he had the students taste the sassafras leaves. Some comments about root beer were heard. Then David took a double handful of sweet-shrubs and crushed them. As he walked down each row of students letting every student smell them, the students "oohed" and "aahed." Next, David gave each student a leaf from a cherry tree. He asked them to break the leaves in half and sniff them to see who could tell him the type of tree these leaves came from. Some said that they smelled like a milkshake. Others said the smell reminded them of the chocolate-covered cherry candy that they get at Christmas. After a wisecrack guess that it was a Christmas tree, someone screamed "cherry."

Next, David had some yellow roots. He asked each student to take a small hair of the root and taste it. They were as bitter as quinine. Students gasped in exaggerated disapproval of the bitter taste; some ran to the door and spat outside. By the end of the period every student was grappling with a piece of sugar cane, twisting it and swallowing the sweet juice.

When the bell rang the students applauded and commented about the lesson. Some said that this is the way school ought to be—fun. David was pleased that the students received the lesson so well.

Dr. Ahrens realized that he had become so engaged with observing the activities and so bewildered and upset at having seen something that didn't even resemble a lesson that he had failed to complete the rating instrument and was, therefore, unprepared for the assessment conference that was to follow. Nevertheless, he felt that he must give David some badly needed feedback, however general. He would spare no words for this young maverick.

Dr. Ahrens's first step toward resolving this perceived disaster was to meet with Mr. Bob Smith, David's cooperating teacher. After sharing a few brief pleasantries he fired the following questions at Mr. Smith.

"What do you think about this lesson?"

"The kids were really excited over it."

"Would you say that this was typical of David's lessons?"

"Yes, he always gets the students fired up."

"Do you think the lesson was well structured, well planned?"

"He obviously kept things moving at a good pace, and he didn't run out of material," Bob Smith answered.

"Does David usually give you a well-prepared lesson plan when he teaches?"

"David has the type of personality that enables him to move through the lesson well without a written plan. I think lesson plans are good if you need them, but they can handicap a natural teacher. David knows that as long as his lessons work, I really don't insist on seeing a written lesson plan," Bob Smith stated.

From this brief conversation Dr. Ahrens concluded that he would get little help from this lackadaisical teacher. In fact, he assumed that Mr. Smith was influencing David negatively by providing a loose, unstructured role model. Clearly, it was time to talk to David.

Dr. Ahrens began the session by asking David what he thought he was doing. He continued, "I drove two hundred miles to watch you teach, and instead you provided a circus. My job is to help you raise the achievement scores in this class. From our prestudent teaching seminar you learned that effective teachers give clear goals, hold high expectations, use direct instruction, and closely supervise all assignments. Instead of following this instructional model, you arranged for a disorganized, student-centered picnic, complete with refreshments. I am very disappointed. I will have to record these activities and place the report in your permanent records."

David was shocked. What could he do to salvage his student-teaching grade and his teaching career?

THE CHALLENGE: Put yourself in David's place. What would you do?

KEY ISSUES FOR STUDY

1. Is it professional behavior for a teacher to engage students in activities such as sniffing leaves and eating sugarcane?

2. What are some potential liabilities of providing such activities?

3. List some advantages of providing such student activities.

4. Can a teacher be too enthusiastic? Explain.

5. Is there evidence suggesting that David's selection of the school for his student teaching contributed to his problem? If so, how?

6. When teachers break away from the everyday routine way of teaching, such as changing the location of the class (field trips) or changing to different teaching methods, what types of precautions can they take to minimize the possible criticism?

7. In general, does increased teacher freedom imply increased teacher responsibilities? Explain.

8. What can teachers do to assure that students learn from experiential lessons?

9. Examine the following steps given in Porter and Brophy's model for effective teachers and identify any steps that David omitted. According to Porter and Brophy (1988) effective teachers:

a. are clear about their instructional goals

b. are knowledgeable about their content and the strategies for teaching it

c. communicate to their students what is expected of them—and why

d. make expert use of existing instructional materials in order to devote more time to practices that enrich and clarify the content

e. are knowledgeable about their students, adapting instruction to their needs and anticipating misconceptions in their existing knowledge

f. teach students metacognitive strategies and give them opportunities to master them

g. address higher- as well as lower-level cognitive objectives

h. monitor students' understanding by offering regular appropriate feedback

i. integrate their instruction with that in other subject areas

j. accept responsibility for student outcomes

k. are thoughtful and reflective about their practice

SUGGESTED READINGS

Bettencourt, E. M., Gillett, M. H., Gall, M. D., & Hull, R. E. (1983). The effects of teacher enthusiasm training on student on-task behavior and achievement. *American Educational Research Journal, 20*, 435–450.

Birnie, H. H., & Ryan, A. (1984). Inquiry/discovery revisited. *Science and Children, 21*, 31–32.

Duley, J. S., & Permaul, J. S. (1984). Participation and benefits from experiential education. *Educational Record, 65*, 18–21.

Gerlovich, J. A. (1983). Avoiding negligence suits in chemistry teaching. *The Physics Teacher, 21*, 368.

Henson, Kenneth, T. (1986). Inquiry learning: A new look. *Contemporary Education, 62*(4), 181–183.

Isaksen, S. G., & Parnes, S. J. (1985). Curriculum planning for creative thinking and problem solving. *Journal of Creative Behavior, 19*(1), 1–29.

Jacobs, L. B. (1985). Education, Jake's way: Discover the wonders of a walking trip. *Early Years, 16*, 78.

Kyle, W. C., Jr. (1985). What research says: Science through discovery: Students love it. *Science and Children, 23*, 39–41.

Liebeck, P. (1986). In defense of experience. *Mathematics Teaching, 114*, 36–38.

Lovedahl G. G., & Tesolowski, D. G. (1986). Planning and conducting effective field trips. *The Technology Teacher, 45*, 27–29.

Porter, A., & Brophy, J. (1988). Synthesis of research on good teaching. *Educational Leadership, 45*, 74–85.

Scott, L. C. (1983). Injury in the classroom: Are teachers liable? *Young Children, 38*, 10–18.

Sheilngold, K. (1987). Keeping children's knowledge alive through inquiry. *School Library Media Quarterly, 15*, 80–85.

Smith L. J., & Smith, D. L. (1986). Experiential learning: Teaching teachers to transfer their knowledge. *Journal of Reading, 29*, 342–345.

Van Cleaf, D. W. (1984). Guiding student inquiry. *Social Studies, 75*, 109–111.

Zirkel, P. A., & Gluckman, I. B. (1984). Liability for off-site inquiries. *Principal, 63*, 47–48.

CASE 7

Asking the Teacher to Evaluate the Principal

THE COMMUNITY

Rolling Meadows is a suburban community approximately twenty-five miles from one of the largest cities in the United States. With a population of 12,400, the average family income is 35 percent above the state average. Nearly 70 percent of the adult population has graduated from college. Virtually all of the homes have been built in the past twenty-five years, and most of the families have lived there less than ten years. A growing number of residents in this affluent town are referred to as DINCS—dual incomes, no children.

THE SCHOOL DISTRICT

Rolling Meadows contains three elementary schools (K–5), a middle school (6–8), and a high school (9–12). The district's boundaries are contiguous with those of the town of Rolling Meadows. The district is governed by a seven-member school board consisting of a physician, a furniture store owner, a college professor, two housewives, a foreman in a manufacturing plant, and an engineer. All are elected to the board. The superintendent is Dr. Anne Davis, who is in her fourth year as the chief executive, having served as a teacher and principal in Rolling Meadows for nineteen years prior to becoming superintendent. She is assisted in the central office by Mr. George Canlon, business manager. Dr. Davis is respected for her work in curriculum development, and she maintains close contact with each of the five schools in the system. Being single, Dr. Davis devotes an unusually high number of hours to her job.

THE SCHOOL AND SCHOOL LEADERSHIP

Rolling Meadows Middle School was erected in 1979. It is a luxurious facility offering outstanding laboratories and support equipment for a middle school. With an enrollment of 654 students, it offers a broad curriculum. The school has become especially well known for its mathematics and science programs. The principal of the school, Mr. Kendrick, was employed by a former superintendent when the school opened. He is well liked by staff and parents, but he is not perceived as an instructional leader by Dr. Davis and several of the faculty. Mr. Kendrick is most effective in human relations. He is a good-natured extrovert. Several teachers in the school have become close personal friends with Mr. Kendrick and his wife.

THE TEACHER

Walter McBain is a first-year teacher who graduated from a state-supported research institution with a major in earth science and a minor in biology. His student teaching was completed in a large urban junior high school. His college grades were excellent (A−) and his performance in student teaching resulted in a rating of "outstanding." Walter grew up in a small farming community in central Illinois. He vowed that he would never return to a rural area because of the limited social and cultural opportunities. He is engaged to a stock broker he met while attending college. Walter has been friendly with other faculty members, but he is perceived as a "loner." His contact with other professionals in the school is quite limited. His principal views him as a hard worker. Walter takes his professional responsibilities very seriously. He is determined to excel in teaching; he wants to be known as the best teacher in the school district. Walter believes in himself; he thinks he is destined to become a truly outstanding teacher.

THE INCIDENT

In early November in a conversation with a colleague, Walter expressed disappointment that Mr. Kendrick did not visit his classroom, exhibited little interest in his teaching endeavors, and offered no instructional supervision.

Walter said, "I really expected that a school with such a positive reputation would have a principal actively involved in helping teachers with their instructional responsibilities. I want a strong leader who can help me in my first years of teaching."

It did not take long for these comments to make their way to Mr. Kendrick and the entire faculty. Walter was viewed as a "troublemaker" by some of the older teachers who supported Mr. Kendrick's laissez-faire style of leadership. Although Mr. Kendrick did not confront Walter about the comments, he did express negative feelings concerning the situation to other teachers and several parents.

He told one parent, "I'm not sure Mr. McBain has what it takes to be a good teacher at this school. If your child has any problems with him, you just let met know. I'm keeping an eye on him."

As might be expected in a small suburban community, the details of this conflict soon made their way to Dr. Davis. Right before the Christmas break, she called Walter and informed him that he was to come to her office for a conference the next day. Although Walter had met Dr. Davis when he was hired and he had seen her visit the school on numerous occasions, he did not know her well. Walter inquired as to the reason for the conference.

"Oh, I just want to talk to you about how you're doing in your first year of teaching," she replied.

When Walter arrived for the conference the next day, he received a warm greeting. Dr. Davis offered him a cup of coffee and exchanged a few pleasantries.

She inquired, "You didn't tell Mr. Kendrick you were coming to see me, did you?" He replied that he had not. "Good," she said. "Walter, I think we have a serious problem at the middle school. Several of the teachers at the school—the ones I really trust—tell me you are an excellent first-year teacher. Further, I understand that your relationship with Mr. Kendrick may not be the best. Is that true?"

"As far as I'm concerned," Walter said, "my relationship with him is fine. I just wish he would show more interest in my teaching and professional development."

Dr. Davis smiled, "Walter, I share that concern. He's a popular principal, but that popularity doesn't necessarily mean that he is an effective principal. The school has a good reputation because there are good teachers there; it's a fine facility and the students come from good homes. But the school is not improving. Kendrick isn't doing anything to help it improve."

Walter sat and listened. He wondered why Dr. Davis was being so candid with him.

After several other comments reflecting upon Mr. Kendrick's performance as principal, Dr. Davis said, "Walter, I want you to help me with something. I'm trying to convince the school board that Mr. Kendrick is not doing the types of things a good principal should be doing. Of course, the board will not be swayed easily. They hear many positive comments about Kendrick from parents and teachers. But people praise him because he is a 'backslapper.' He doesn't demand much of himself or others. We are going to be having an executive session of the school board next Tuesday night. I'd like you to come to that meeting and tell the board how disappointed you are that you don't have a principal who is providing leadership. People know you're a good teacher. Your view will make a difference. Will you do that?"

THE CHALLENGE: You are Walter. What is your decision? How do you respond to Dr. Davis?

KEY ISSUES FOR STUDY:

1. Evaluate the merits of Walter making comments about his principal. Should Walter have said anything about his principal in the first place? Explain your answer.

2. Evaluate Walter's expectations of his principal. Do you agree that you would want a principal who would work closely with you on instructional matters? Defend your response.

3. Identify contributing factors that may be Walter's fault.

4. Should Walter have told Mr. Kendrick that Dr. Davis wanted to see him? Why or why not?

5. Identify additional information you would have wanted in order to decide upon a course of action in this case.

6. Identify information that is not relevant to reaching a decision.

7. Identify the positive and negative aspects of Walter agreeing to cooperate with Dr. Davis.

8. Identify the positive and negative aspects of Walter refusing to cooperate with Dr. Davis.

SUGGESTED READINGS

Evans, D. (1986). Leadership misconstrued: The myth of "super principal." *Thrust*, *15*, 37–39.

Haberman, M. (1985). Can common sense effectively guide the behavior of beginning teachers? *Journal of Teacher Education, 36*(6), 32–35.

Johnston, G. S., & Venable, B. P. (1986). A study of teacher loyalty to the principal: Rule administration and hierarchical influence of the principal. *Educational Administration Quarterly, 22*(4), 4–27.

Lieberman, A., & Miller, L. (1984). The social realities of teaching. *Teachers, Their World, Their Work*, (pp. 1–16). Alexandria, VA: Association for Supervision and Curriculum Development.

Robinson, G. E., & Protheroe, N. (1986). The teachers speak out. *Principal, 65* (7), 58–60.

Questioning in the Classroom

As they rode back to their school, the four Belmont teachers compared notes on the afternoon inservice.

"Professor Brooks really knew her stuff," Jayne Broderick remarked enthusiastically. "I'm not easily impressed by inservices, but there were several activities I observed today that I can integrate into my science teaching."

"What made it for me was the way she used those three teachers from Cranston to illustrate questioning techniques. That made it so much more realistic," commented Jessie Crane. "And the fact that one of them was a home economics teacher like me made it even better."

"I understand that Professor Brooks has been working with the teachers at Cranston for several months. Some kind of grant from the state department of education," Henry Carlyle added.

"I had forgotten about Sanders's *Classroom Questions* and Bloom's *Taxonomy*. They've been collecting dust in my bookcase at home since I finished my social studies methods class. I'd forgotten how useful they could be," Robert Benson said.

"We used them too in my English methods course at Tech," noted Mr. Carlyle.

"In an NSF summer institute a few years ago I remember having to prepare instructional goals and related questions, using the taxonomy," Mrs. Broderick said.

"I'm going to take another look at some of the materials I have at home on questioning techniques," Mr. Benson said as he steered the car into the Belmont parking lot.

"Thanks for driving today," Mrs. Broderick said.

"Yes, we appreciate it," Mrs. Crane agreed. "First-year teachers don't always get stuck driving."

The teachers laughed.

Robert Benson parked his car and let the other teachers out. As they departed, each offered the others wishes for an enjoyable weekend.

Benson pulled from the parking space, drove out of the lot, and headed toward his apartment a few miles away. As he drove, he thought about his seven weeks of teaching at Belmont. He recalled how suprised he had been, when he interviewed for the job, that seven native languages are spoken by Belmont students. Having grown up in a small, rural town and having had attended a school enrolling 656 students in grades seven through twelve, he had been awed by the 2,227 students at Belmont and the massive, block-long brick complex that housed them. He had been shocked by plainclothes security guards in the school. Having come from nearly an all-white community, he had viewed teaching in a school composed of 62 percent black, 26 percent Hispanic, 7 percent Asian, 4 percent white, and 1 percent Native American students with both excitement and fear. In a short time, however, he had become comfortable working in a multiethnic school in an urban community. He felt there were so many cultural advantages to teaching in such a setting.

Four of his five teaching assignments had gone well. He felt fortunate to have three preparations—two in different periods of American history and one in geography. Although he considered his classes to be large from his own school experience, having between thirty and thirty-five students is the norm in basic subjects at Belmont.

The geography class presents the most difficulty, even though Benson feels he can communicate effectively with the thirty-one students. The student composition of the class reflects that of the school. There are eighteen black, seven Hispanic, four Asian, and two white students in the class. The class is an elective at Belmont as a part of social studies requirements. The range of abilities in the class is wide. A fourth of the students are B+ to A students in all course work. More than half are C students. The remainder are D students. Generally, the students are well behaved.

Finding instructional resources is no problem. Benson has been able to find a varied selection of films, filmstrips, slides, and other materials concerning climate, imports and exports, transportation systems, social, economic, and political conditions of the countries being studied. "The students are attentive. I just can't get them to think," he mumbled aloud. "Perhaps attending the conference was a good omen," he thought as he pulled into the parking lot next to the apartment complex where he lived. "Maybe I should spend more time on questioning and less time on lecturing and using audiovisuals."

He got out of his car, locked the door, and walked to apartment 3B. He inserted the key in the door lock, grabbed three letters from his mailbox, opened the door, and entered his apartment. He nudged the door shut with his foot while glancing at the mail. "Just more bills," he grumbled, as he tossed the letters on top of the desk. He unzipped his jacket, took it off, and threw it on the couch. He undid his tie as he walked to the kitchen. As he opened the refrigerator door with one hand, he tossed his tie onto the kitchen table. He pulled out a diet soda, snapped open the top, and sipped from the can. As he continued drinking, he walked back into the living room to a bookcase.

"I know they're here somewhere," he thought. Spying a tattered paperback copy of Bloom's *Taxonomy of Educational Objectives* near the top of the shelf, he pulled it out.

"If I were organized, I'd find Sanders's book close by," he mused.

"Ah, here," he said aloud, as he noticed the book on the bottom shelf between *Yeager* and *Collected Short Stories of Mark Twain*.

He walked to his desk, put his drink down, and began leafing through Sanders's *Classroom Questions: What Kinds?* An excerpt from page 7 caught his eye.

> The taxonomy of questions helps to clarify "learning by doing" by demonstrating that a child can be sitting quietly at a desk and yet be vigorously engaged in any one of a number of kinds of mental activities.

"Just the opposite of my geography class," he thought. "They sit quietly at their desks but aren't really engaged mentally."

He took a sharp pencil and legal-sized yellow pad from the desk drawer and took notes.

In short order he opened Bloom's text. He skimmed over introductory remarks, a discussion of purposes for developing the taxonomy, to the appendix. "Here it is," he remarked. He copied the levels of the taxonomy on a second sheet of paper.

He closed Bloom's book and reopened the Sanders text, went back to the first sheet of paper, and continued writing.

During the weekend, Benson reworked his lesson plan for his fifth-period geography class. He reviewed notes on a twenty-minute UNESCO film on the economic system of Mexico. Then he drew a grid of the taxonomy with each level noted down the left-hand margin of the paper. As he went back over his notes, he wrote questions for each level of the taxonomy. On Monday morning, after getting dressed and eating breakfast, he reworked the questions for a last time, realizing there would not be time during the day to do more planning for the class.

Thirty minutes before the first bell, Benson packed his materials, left the apartment, and drove to Belmont. Up to the fifth period the day went smoothly. Students in each of his classes had been attentive. The level of student participation was higher than usual—particularly for a Monday. He anticipated the geography class with confidence and enthusiasm. He had spent several hours preparing the questions and was excited about trying out his sequenced approach to questioning.

The fifth-period bell rang, and the students took their seats. Benson looked over the names in his grade book and glanced around the room. All the students were present.

For the first five minutes of the class he reviewed Friday's lesson, which had covered the political system in Mexico. After summarizing major points of the political system, Benson set the stage for the class's activity.

"For the remainder of the period," he continued, "we will explore the economic system of Mexico. To introduce the topic I have printed five key terms on the chalkboard. Please put these in your notes.

"As you view the short film I will show in a minute," he continued, "each of these terms will be defined and discussed. Please define the terms in your own words in your notes. Some of the terms you should recognize—we've used them before."

He then repeated the key terms aloud: "Currency. Gold standard. Inflation. Balance of trade. Consumption."

"Mona, please turn off the lights," Benson said as he motioned to a student to ready the room for the film.

After the film, he turned off the projector and flipped on the lights.

"Take the next couple of minutes to finish your notes while I rewind the film and put it in its cannister," Benson instructed the class.

Three minutes later, armed with questions he had prepared over the weekend, Benson began the discussion.

"You will recall that when we studied other countries, we talked about the fact the a country's currency serves as the foundation for its economic system. What is a currency?"

None of the students responded. He waited. After a half-minute of silence, he said impatiently:

"Come on, we've covered this in three other South American countries in the past two weeks. What is a currency?"

Meekly, one of the students offered a response.

"That's a good start," Benson replied reassuringly. "Who can build on what Lois has said?"

For the next thirty minutes Benson struggled to get students to respond. He stumbled through the grid of questions, noticing that students seemed reluctant to offer answers and had trouble moving up the taxonomy to higher-order questions. Out of frustration he ended the discussion early. "We'll continue this tomorrow. Until the end of the period I want you to read pages 123 to 130, your assignment for tomorrow," Benson concluded.

He walked to his desk, sat down, and retraced his steps through the questioning process. He reviewed his list of questions. "What did I do wrong," he wondered.

After class, Benson went to the teachers' lounge—a place he often went to plan, grade papers, or discuss teaching strategies with Dolores Whitney, a forty-three-year-old social studies teacher he considered his mentor. He had met Dolores at a state social studies conference while he was student-teaching a year earlier. She was already in the lounge, putting grades in her grade book.

As Benson entered, Dolores greeted him. "Hello, Bob. How are you?"

"Not so good," Benson responded glumly.

"It shows," Dolores said. "A bad class?"

"I'm not sure what the trouble is. But, yes, the geography class last period was difficult. Especially after all the work I did this weekend to prepare."

"Tell me about it," Dolores remarked.

Benson related his excitement about the Friday inservice, explained the preparation he had made for the class, and reviewed what had happened.

Benson appreciated the fact that Mrs. Whitney was a patient listener. He had come to respect her for her unwillingness to give immediate advice and for her insistence that he think of alternative solutions for instructional problems he faced. Accordingly, he was not surprised when she asked:

"What are you going to do?"

THE CHALLENGE: What *can* Benson do to make the use of higher-order questions a more constructive, successful activity?

KEY ISSUES FOR STUDY:

1. Assume Benson's role. From the information provided, what reasons might you give for the lack of success of the introduction of higher-order questions in the geography class?
2. What additional information would be useful in trying to identify reasons for his lack of success?
3. What other resources might you consult to secure a better understanding of what might have gone wrong?
4. What actions would you plan for Tuesday in geography class to continue the use of higher-order questions?
5. For each action you recommend in item 4, what theory can you offer in support?
6. What information in this case is not relevant to making changes for the effective use of higher-order questioning techniques?

SUGGESTED READINGS

Bloom, B. (Ed.). (1956). *Taxonomy of educational objectives. Handbook I: Cognitive domain*. New York: David McKay.

Ciardiello, A. (1986). Teacher questioning and student interaction: An observation of three social studies classes. *Social Studies*, 77, 119–122.

Check, J. (1985). Fielding and initiating questions in class. *Clearing House, 58,* 270–273.

Daines, D. (1986). Are teachers asking higher level questions? *Education, 106,* 368–374.

Dean, D. (1986). Questioning techniques for teachers: A closer look at the process. *Contemporary Education, 57,* 184–185.

Dillon, J. (1984). Research on questioning and discussion. *Educational Leadership, 42*(3), 50–56.

Farrar, M. (1986). Teacher questions: The complexity of the cognitively simple. *Instructional Science, 15*(2), 89–107.

Felton, R., & Allen, R. (1986). Building questioning skills. *Social Education, 50,* 544–548.

Gall, M. (1984). Synthesis of research on teachers's questioning. *Educational Leadership, 42*(3), 40–47.

Goldman, L. (1984). Warning: The Socratic method can be dangerous. *Educational Leadership, 42,* 57–65.

Harris, P., & Swick, K. (1985). Improving teacher communications: Focus on clarity and questioning skills. *Clearing House, 59,* 13–15.

Kusimo, S., & Erlandson, D. (1983). Instructional communications in a large high school. *NASSP Bulletin, 67,* 18–24.

Nessel, D. (1987). The new face of comprehension instruction: A closer look at questions. *The Reading Teacher, 10*(7), 601–606.

Perez, S. (1986). Improving learning through student questioning. *Clearing House, 60,* 63–65.

Sanders, N. (1966). *Classroom questions: What Kinds?* New York: Harper & Row.

Sheingold, K. (1987). Keeping children's knowledge alive through inquiry. *School Library Media Quarterly, 15*(2), 80–85.

Van Cleaf, D. (1984). Guiding student inquiry. *Social Studies, 75,* 109–111.

Who Goes Where?
Organizing Students
for Instruction

Shelly had not expected to get a full-time teaching position. She had married during the summer and planned to do part-time substituting. She and her husband, a computer engineer, had felt that part-time employment would provide flexibility for their adjustment to marriage and, at the same time, bring in additional income.

One week before the start of school they were surprised when the personnel director from City District called to see if Shelly would be interested in teaching a combined fifth and sixth grade at Woodrow Wilson Elementary. City District is an elementary district within a large urban school corporation. Over the past two decades it has experienced an influx of minorities. What was once considered an elitist, white collar community has become a melting pot. While the makeup of the population has changed dramatically, the reputation of City District as a center of educational excellence has not changed. The "white flight" that occurred in the community was not followed by a similar exodus among teachers. The "aging" faculty has held firm to high expectations for students, a major reason why the district has retained its reputation.

At the same time, civic support for facilities and activities has not waned. Community organizations continue to hold fund-raisers to generate additional funds for the district. During the last twelve years, two tax referendums passed, due largely to the active political support from these civic organizations. Large crowds at sporting events and fine-arts performances illustrate the level of community support.

Woodrow Wilson, the oldest of six elementary schools in the district, opened to 470 students in 1917. Refurbished in 1937, 1954, and again in 1980, the school's traditional brick, factorylike face had been carefully maintained. Currently, the school serves 730 students. Additions have been added to accommodate the expanded student population without sacrificing the architectural character of the building.

Shelly and her husband discussed the opportunity and decided she should sign a contract. There were several reasons for the decision. Shelly had already been processed to be placed on the substitute list; hence, she would not need to request transcripts, fill out forms, and be interviewed. She had completed early field experiences at Woodrow Wilson while she was a sophomore. The principal and several staff who knew her recommended Shelly for the job. Woodrow Wilson was a five-minute drive from their apartment and on the way to her husband's place of work. The thought of having more than twice the income they might have otherwise meant they would have money to buy some luxuries or to invest. The only negative thought was having to take over the job from Deanna Bailey on such short notice.

Shelly knew Deanna Bailey from her university days. She had observed the veteran teacher on several occasions. She remembered Mrs. Bailey as a demanding, highly organized, creative teacher. Shelly felt pressure, knowing that within three working days she would have to be prepared to teach twenty-eight fifth and sixth graders from highly diverse backgrounds.

Shelly had met with Elicia Fernandez, principal at Wilson, and learned that Mrs. Bailey would probably not return. She had become seriously ill during the summer and prognosis for full recovery was not good. In typical fashion Mrs. Bailey had worked until the day before surgery. She had prepared a list of the names of the twenty-eight students and had typed a brief description of what she knew about them. Shelly found these materials in a folder she was given. She read a few of the descriptions.

- EDUARDO RUIZ, grade 5, has three brothers and two sisters—all older than he. His father is a factory worker and his mother cleans houses. None of his brothers and sisters has graduated from high school, although all of them range in age from twenty-three to twenty-nine. "Eddie," as his friends call him, is an outgoing, alert, verbal child. He is viewed as somewhat of a clown. He rarely misses school and seems to like everyone. His grandparents came to the United States from Uruguay as seasonal farm workers.

- LATANA JUAREZ, grade 5, is an only child. She is supported by her mother, who works two jobs—during the day as a waitress in a restaurant and at night as a security guard. Latana sees her mother for a couple of hours each night and, otherwise, is left alone during the week. Sometimes on weekends her mother also must work. Latana is shy and introverted, has few friends, and has a spotty attendance record.

- LUCINDA BROWN, grade 5, is the child of a mixed marriage. "Candy," as her friends call her both because of her sweet disposition and her mother's occupation, has a Caucasian father and an Afro-American mother. Her father runs a barber shop in the community, while her mother sells homemade candy marketed from their house. Candy is a bubbly, fun-loving child. She enjoys reading mystery stories and writing poetry. She is viewed by others as creative.

- HENRY CHIN, grade 5, is one of two children who has been supported by his mother. His father was killed in the Vietnam War. His older brother is a computer salesman on the East Coast. He rarely sees or hears from his brother. His mother works as a seamstress for a clothing manufacturer. Henry skips school frequently. When he does, he tries to sneak into movie theaters in the neighborhood. He spends much of his time in front of a screen—either movie or television. He is an aggressive, loud child who gets angry when he does not get his way.

- MALLORY APPLEGATE, grade 5, is a frail, only child. She was born six weeks prematurely. Her father is a Methodist minister; her mother a stenographer for an insurance company. Mallory, because of continuing ill health, has few friends. Her peers have given her the nickname "Malaria." She daydreams often. She has a short attention span, is easily brought to tears, and is absent regularly because of illness.

- RONNIE CHANG, grade 6, is an only child. He lives with his grandparents, both of whom are now retired and in their late sixties. His mother is deceased. Ronnie's father is an industrial plant supervisor in Taiwan. During the summer months, Ronnie returns to Taiwan to spend time with his father. He wishes that he lived with his father. Often he appears depressed. He does not mix easily with his peers. He argues often with his grandparents. He frequently misses school and hangs out with a junior high school gang called the "Kings." Ronnie enjoys rock music. He owns an electric guitar and is teaching himself to play.

- CARLOTA OVANDO, grade 6, is one of three sisters. One sister—seven years older—is a senior in high school but may not graduate because she does not have the required number of credits. Another sister— three years older—is thinking about dropping out of school. She currently holds a part-time job washing dishes in a restaurant. Carlota's father is an upholsterer and her mother is a cook at a mission for the homeless. Carlota missed two years of school while the family traveled through the West and Midwest doing seasonal farm work. Carlota has been told she must begin thinking of ways she can help the family. Her parents want her to look for a job. Carlota enjoys reading and thinks she would like to be a newspaper reporter someday.

5TH AND 6TH GRADE CLASS

							GRADE EQUIVALENTS Iowa Tests of Basic Skills									
Student's Names	Age	C	V	R	La	Lb	Lc	Ld	L	Wa	Wb	W	Ma	Mb	Mc	M
GRADE 5																
M/H Eduardo Ruiz	12	4.2	4.2	3.8	4.0	4.3	4.2	4.1	4.2	3.8	4.2	4.0	4.1	4.3	4.0	4.1
F/H Latana Juarez	10	4.1	4.3	4.2	3.4	5.0	4.4	3.3	4.0	2.2	5.9	4.0	4.1	4.3	3.1	3.8
M/AF James Hightower	10	4.6	6.0	6.9	5.0	4.8	5.6	6.3	5.4	5.7	5.3	5.5	4.2	4.7	4.4	4.4
M/C Edward Flaherty	10	4.2	4.2	4.6	4.5	3.9	4.4	5.5	4.6	4.0	3.8	3.9	3.7	3.2	3.6	3.5
F/AF Lucinda Brown	10	6.1	6.1	7.5	6.4	5.0	6.2	8.5	6.5	7.7	6.9	7.3	5.2	5.5	5.1	5.3
M/AF Eddie Smith	10	5.5	5.5	4.5	6.4	5.0	5.6	6.5	5.9	5.9	6.4	6.2	5.2	5.8	5.4	5.5
M/C Henry Newar	11	6.8	7.2	6.7	5.4	6.4	4.2	6.5	5.6	6.3	5.3	5.8	6.2	7.2	5.2	6.2
M/AR Abdullah Al-Baran	10	6.4	6.6	7.1	5.6	5.5	7.5	7.1	6.4	5.4	6.6	6.0	6.2	7.2	5.5	6.3
M/AS Henry Chin	10	3.9	4.4	4.7	3.7	3.3	3.2	4.8	3.8	2.8	3.4	3.1	3.4	3.6	3.3	3.4
M/AS Rudy Tatupu	10	6.0	6.0	6.9	6.4	5.0	5.3	6.8	5.9	5.8	6.4	6.0	6.5	6.3	4.3	5.8
F/C Mallory Applegate	10	5.1	5.1	5.3	5.9	4.8	4.4	5.8	5.2	5.4	2.2	3.3	4.1	3.6	4.3	4.0
F/H Maria Notchez	10	5.1	6.6	5.2	5.8	4.1	6.5	5.8	5.6	5.1	6.0	5.6	5.6	4.3	4.8	4.9
M/H Roberto Feliz	10	6.2	6.3	7.3	5.0	6.0	5.6	5.3	5.5	6.3	6.6	6.0	5.9	5.8	5.5	5.7
F/AF Yolanda Smith	9	6.1	6.3	6.7	5.8	5.5	6.8	6.3	6.6	5.0	7.2	6.1	5.9	5.2	4.8	5.3
GRADE 6																
M/AS Ronnie Chang	11	5.0	5.2	4.9	3.7	4.4	4.8	4.5	4.4	6.1	5.1	5.6	5.8	4.3	4.9	5.0
F/H Carlota Ovando	13	6.4	6.7	7.7	6.4	6.0	6.5	6.1	6.3	6.7	5.6	6.3	4.2	5.8	4.8	4.9
F/AF Cindy LaVerne	11	5.0	5.0	5.6	5.0	4.8	5.5	5.1	5.1	3.3	6.1	4.7.	3.8	4.9	5.6	4.8

Student	Grade															
F/AS Alvina Ming	11	7.1	6.7	7.7	8.1	7.3	7.2	5.6	7.1	6.9	5.6	6.8	9.0	6.8	5.6	7.3
M/AS Hoji Hikawa	11	8.0	7.8	8.9	8.1	5.8	8.2	7.8	7.5	8.5	7.8	8.2	7.9	7.6	6.9	7.5
F/C Jennifer Jensen	11	7.6	6.9	7.7	8.6	8.1	7.2	9.7	8.4	9.0	7.6	8.3	7.5	7.3	5.8	6.9
M/AF Luther Bradford	12	7.6	7.5	7.9	6.1	6.7	6.2	6.7	6.4	9.0	8.3	8.7	7.7	8.0	6.9	7.5
M/C John Jones	11	7.2	8.1	6.4	6.8	6.7	7.2	7.5	7.1	7.4	6.9	7.2	8.1	7.6	6.6	7.2
M/H Edwardo Flavo	11	7.4	7.8	7.7	7.2	8.5	7.9	8.6	8.1	7.9	5.6	6.8	7.3	7.3	5.9	6.8
F/H Lisa Puerta	12	8.0	8.4	8.4	7.8	6.0	7.2	9.1	7.5	9.2	8.3	8.8	7.2	7.0	6.9	7.0
M/AF Lew Benson	11	7.4	6.9	7.5	7.4	6.3	8.2	7.8	7.4	7.8	8.3	8.1	7.5	7.6	6.5	7.2
M/H Juan Salizar	11	7.5	6.7	8.1	8.9	8.8	9.1	6.4	8.3	6.5	6.0	6.3	7.9	8.0	8.0	8.0
F/AF Carrie Evans	11	5.5	5.5	4.4	5.9	5.0	5.9	5.6	5.6	5.8	5.5	5.7	6.1	6.4	5.7	6.1
M/C Tom Rose	11	7.9	8.1	7.9	9.2	8.5	9.1	7.5	8.6	7.4	7.3	7.4	6.6	9.4	5.8	6.1

GRADE EQUIVALENTS

The scale for grade equivalents ranges from 0.0 through 12.9 representing the 13 years of school (K-12) and the 10 months in the traditional school year. September is viewed as the start of the year (.0) October is identified as .1, November as .2, and so forth to June (.9). A grade equivalent represents the grade and month in school of students in the norm group whose test performance is theoretically equivalent to the test performance of a given student.

STUDENT CODE

C=Composite
V=Vocabulary
R=Reading
La=Spelling
Lb=Capitalization
Lc=Punctuation
L=Language (total)
Wa=Visual
Wb=References
Wc=Work/study (total)
Ma=Math concepts
Mb=Math problems
Mc=Math computation
M=Math (total)

M/AF=Male/Afro-American
F/AF=Female/Afro-American
M/AR=Male/Arab
F/AR=Female/Arab
M/AS=Male/Asian
F/AS=Female/Asian
M/C=Male/Caucasian
F/C=Female/Caucasian
M/H=Male/Hispanic
F/H=Female/Hispanic

Figure 9.1. Summary of test skills for the Iowa Tests of Basic Skills

- HOJI HIKAWA, grade 6, is the only son of a Japanese family that immigrated to the United States five years ago. When he came to America he spoke little English but has made rapid progress. His father is an assembly line foreman and his mother works in the home and occasionally baby-sits. Hoji is a sports enthusiast. His favorite sport is judo. He takes judo lessons every Thursday night and every Saturday morning. He is outgoing and gets along well with other children. He enjoys all subjects in school.

- JENNIFER JENSEN, grade 6, is an adopted child who lives with a divorced mother, who had no other children. Her mother is a salesperson for a cosmetics manufacturer and, on occasion, must travel for several days at a time. During her absence, Jennifer stays with a next-door family of five. The neighbors have two children, both in college, and a grandmother living in the home. Jennifer enjoys the opportunity to stay with the family. Jennifer is athletic and enjoys swimming and running. She also enjoys history.

- LISA PUERTA, grade 6, is the older of two children. She has a sister who is two months old. Her father owns and operates a large machinery repair business. Her mother is a bookkeeper in the business. Lisa and her sister spend most evenings after school in the office area of the business, where their parents work until after ten most nights. Her mother has taught Lisa many of the bookkeeping tasks and has permitted her to do some of the math work required for keeping financial records. Lisa enjoys spending time at the business because she gets to meet so many different people. Lisa is an outgoing, highly verbal girl who makes friends easily. She enjoys reading fiction.

"These are interesting descriptions," Shelly thought to herself. "I wonder if I can get any other information." As she leafed through the folder, she discovered a summary of test scores on the Iowa Tests of Basic Skills. (See Figure 9.1 on pp. 46–47.)

THE CHALLENGE: What information should Shelly use in order to organize the children for instruction?

KEY ISSUES FOR STUDY:

1. Was it wise for Mrs. Bailey to leave the descriptions of the students along with a summary of test scores? Explain your answer.
2. To what extent will these descriptions influence the way in which the students are organized for instruction? For example,
   a. What would you do to encourage Eduardo Ruiz to take his studies seriously?
   b. Given the fact that Latana Luarez has little contact with either adults or peers,

what would you do to enhance her chances of developing adult and childhood friends? How might you organize instruction to improve her attendance record?

c. As a child from a racially mixed marriage, Lucinda Brown may face ridicule or embarrassment from her classmates. What could you do to prevent such ridicule from occurring? Or, if it did occur, how would you respond to it?

d. Henry Chin has a strong interest in movies and television. In what ways could you use the media to get Henry more interested in school work?

e. Mallory Applegate has already been stigmatized by her peers' behavior toward her. Given her condition and the way she has been treated in the past how would you improve both her social and educational standing in your classroom?

f. Ronnie Chang has substituted gang association for the absence of his father. What can you do to challenge and to influence his gang association and get him excited about classroom instruction?

g. Carlota Ovando's parents hold unrealistic expectations for her. They want her to get a job. She has no successful role models in terms of educational attainment. How could you organize instruction to build on her interests and to also confront the obstacles to long-term educational success imposed by her family situation?

h. Some students appear to be highly motivated. Hoji Hikawa seems to be one of them. What would you do to maintain his high level of motivation?

i. Jennifer Jensen appears to be successful. In time, however, how might her mother's continual, lengthy absences affect Jennifer's classroom behavior? How would you respond?

j. Lisa Puerta has experienced success by virtue of her help in the family business. How can these experiences at home be used in the classroom to enhance her educational success?

3. How can the statistical data provided be used for organizing students for instruction? Explain why these data are useful. What other data might be helpful?

4. Should information be sought from other teachers who may know these students? Defend your answer.

5. Should parents be used as a data source for organizing students for instruction? Explain your answer.

6. In what ways might information from the students themselves be helpful? How would you collect the data?

7. How much data about the students should be collected in order to make an adequate decision for grouping students for instruction?

SUGGESTED READINGS

Gregory, R. P. (1984). Streaming, setting and mixed ability grouping in primary and secondary schools: Some research findings. *Educational Studies*, *10*(3), 209–226.

Haller, E. J., & Waterman, M. (1985). The criteria of reading group assignments. *Reading Teacher*, *38*(8), 772–781.

Jongsma, E. (1985). Grouping for instruction. *Reading Teacher*, *38*(9), 918–920.

Oakes, J. (1986). Keeping track, part 2: Curriculum inequality and school reform. *Phi Delta Kappan*, *68*(2), 148–154.

Pink, W. (1984). Creating effective schools. *Educational Forum*, *49*(1), 91–107.

Powers, S., Escamilla, K., & Haussler, M. et. al. (1986). The California achievement test as a predictor of reading ability across race and sex. *Educational and Psychological Measurement*, *46*(4), 1067–1070.

Riccio, L. L. (1985). Facts and issues about ability grouping. *Contemporary Education*, *57*(1), 26–30.

CASE 10

Rodney Misbehaves

Mansfield, Stacey, and Boonville are three small rural communities that make up the Oak Bloom School District. Mansfield is the smallest of the communities with 723 people. Stacey has 987, and Boonville is the largest with 2,300 inhabitants. The primary economic base in these towns is farming. Approximately 70 percent of the working adults are engaged in agricultural occupations. Most of the remaining working adults are employed by a nearby General Motors plant located in Townsend, a city of 58,000 people. A few black and Hispanic families—most of whom are employed in the auto-manufacturing plant—have moved into the area. Citizens in these three small communities are known traditionally as hard-working, conservative, religious people.

Oak Bloom School District is a consolidation of the three towns. Until five years ago, each town had its own elementary, junior high, and high school. Historically, Mansfield was noted for its home economics and agriculture programs. Few of its graduating seniors went on to postsecondary training. Most stayed and worked in the community. Stacey had a similar history; however, its reputation was built upon outstanding basketball and track teams. In its division Stacey won two state basketball championships and was ranked consistently in state polls. While its track teams never won a state title, the school sent athletes to compete in the state track competition nearly every year. Boonville had a larger number of students attending postsecondary institutions, about 17 percent. Boonville enjoyed a reputation for fine mathematics and music programs. Each of the towns was known for strong support for its programs, high attendance at school events, and a competitive spirit.

The consolidation of the towns into Oak Bloom School District was

51

painful. Each of the towns wanted to maintain its respective identity. During the merger, it was decided to develop a new identity; hence, all of the former mascots and team names were discarded. Given the southern location of the communities in this midwestern state, the new district adopted the nickname of "The Rebels." A Confederate flag now flies alongside both the state and American flags outside the administration building. A junior/senior high building has been constructed two miles east of Boonville. Each of the existing elementary schools continues to operate in the towns.

Frank Zeitz has been the only superintendent in the school district. He was born and raised in the area and is a graduate of Stacey. Upon graduation from college, he returned to teach elementary school for seven years at Boonville Elementary. During this time he completed his administrator's credential and was named principal of the school. He served as principal for five years and completed his superintendent's license. When the consolidation occurred, Zeitz was a logical choice for the job. He has surrounded himself with loyal administrators, most of whom also grew up in the area. Each building principal has autonomy in making decisions. Dr. Zeitz prides himself on being an effective delegator.

Rollin Glenn has been principal of Oak Bloom High for five years. He is known as an administrator with great confidence in his teachers. Accordingly, he allows a high level of teacher participation in decision making. At the same time, he is a team player, loyal to the central administration. Prior to becoming an administrator he had been a basketball coach and athletic director at one of the competing high schools in a neighboring county; hence, he continues to maintain close contact and support for athletic programs. Having been a successful coach, he is respected in the community.

Alice Roberts, twenty-four, is an English, speech, and drama teacher at Oak Bloom High School. This is her first teaching position. She was born in and has lived most of her life in Philadelphia, and is a graduate of the University of Pennsylvania. Between college graduation and employment, she traveled and held down odd jobs so that she could see as much of Europe as possible. She spent four years on the Continent.

She was a B+ student in college and used much of her free time as an advocate for a variety of causes. She served in student government, was a member of a voluntary service group that worked with community social agencies, held office in a countywide nuclear-freeze group, and participated in civic theater performances.

Alice took the job at Oak Bloom to "slow down the pace of life." There were many aspects of big-city living with which she had tired—congested traffic, crime, high housing costs, and high food prices. She had decided that a move to rural America would be good for her.

When she arrived in the community, she rented a turn-of-the-century wood frame house in Stacey. She found the people in Stacey to be warm and friendly. On weekends she attended community gatherings—pancake breakfasts, fish frys, and ice cream socials, went to as many rummage sales as possible, and did volunteer work at the local hospital. In a short time she became an active, welcomed member in the community.

After a few weeks following this routine, Alice grew restless. Compared to her earlier commitment to social and political issues, her hospital work seemed superficial and shallow. She began to yearn for museums, art galleries, a variety of ethnic foods, the symphony, plays and musicals, and voluminous libraries. Gradually, she began to rethink her decision to move to the country.

She was less welcome at Oak Bloom by her peers than she was by community members in Stacey. Nearly all the faculty at Oak Bloom had spent their entire lives in rural communities. They were suspicious of anyone who appeared to be different. Clearly her urban upbringing and travels set her distinctly apart from them. Frank Zeitz had noticed this difference in the initial interview and saw hiring her as a way to begin to build a more balanced faculty. What this difference meant to Alice was that she was largely ignored by the faculty. As time progressed, she became more lonely. She was truly a loner in the school. This fact bothers her, but Alice does not dwell on it. In a way, she feels that being left alone works to her advantage. "I can do what I want to do without having someone watch over me," she thought. As a result, she believes she is better able to give her full attention to teaching.

Alice takes pride in her first-period speech class. She spends countless hours preparing interesting activities for students. She approaches each day with enthusiasm, knowing how important it is to get off to a good start. How her first period goes affects her for the rest of the day. Not all students view Alice's first period speech class with the same enthusiasm.

Rodney McCallum, a black sophomore star football player at the school, has shown the least interest in the class. He missed the first two days of class, but had an excuse from the football coach. He had been soaking an injured ankle in the whirlpool in the athletic training room in the school. He was late to class by two or three minutes on three other occasions during the first three weeks of school, but in each instance he had a written excuse from the coach.

On days when students in the speech class gave short oral presentations Rodney led a group of four other males in the class in heckling the students. These five students made faces at students giving speeches. The heckling was done in such a way that Alice, who sat in the back of the room when students made presentations, was unaware of the students' behavior. After the class, two students reported Rodney's and the other hecklers' behavior to Alice. The next morning, before class, she confronted Rodney.

"I understand you and your friends were making faces at students giving speeches yesterday," she began.

"Who said that?" Rodney asked.

"That is not important. Did you or didn't you make faces?" Alice demanded, her voice increasing in intensity.

"No, I didn't," Rodney responded. "Why are you always giving me a hard time?"

"I'm not giving you a hard time. I want you to pay attention, participate in class, and learn. I care about you," she concluded.

Rodney turned, walked back to his seat, and sat down. As he did, he muttered loud enough so that Alice could hear: "You're prejudiced." Until class began, he placed his face down against his folded arms pressed against the desk top.

On a Thursday during the third week of classes Rodney began mumbling barely audible statements that a few students around him could hear. He said, "This class stinks. Ms. Roberts is ugly." These and other negative comments continued to the point that Alice finally overheard Rodney and his friends chuckling in response to a comment.

She stopped her lecture and asked: "What did you say, Rodney?"

Rodney replied, "I didn't say anything."

"What is so funny?" she asked, again directing her inquiry at Rodney.

"Nothing," Rodney responded.

Alice gave him a stern look, then continued lecturing. After class she expressed her concern about his behavior. She indicated that he had better be more attentive or she would have to take some form of disciplinary action.

At the beginning of Monday's class during the fourth week of school, Alice divided the students into groups of three. She went around the room counting off: "One-two-three, one-two-three, one-two-three." As she did, students were buzzing with anticipation of a small-group activity. When she got to Rodney, he was one of two students left that did not have a group. She pointed to the first student and said, "You're a one." She pointed to Rodney and said, "Rodney, you're a two. And I'll be a three," she concluded. "We can work together."

"No way I'm gonna be in a group with no damn teacher!" Rodney blurted out loudly.

The class became silent.

THE CHALLENGE: You are Alice Roberts. How will you respond to Rodney McCallum's behavior?

KEY ISSUES FOR STUDY:

1. What would you do immediately in response to Rodney's remark?
2. What are possible negative consequences of your response? What are positive consequences?
3. What are the possible causes of Rodney's behavior?
4. What has Alice done that may contribute to Rodney's negative behavior?
5. What are some possible long-term solutions for dealing with Rodney's behavior?

6. What are some actions that Alice might have taken earlier to shape Rodney's behavior?

7. Describe additional information you would have wanted in order to make a decision.

8. Identify information not relevant to making a decision.

SUGGESTED READINGS

Allen, J. D. (1986). Classroom management: Students, perspectives, goals, and strategies. *American Education Research Journal, 23,* 437–459.

Anderson, L., & Prawat, R. (1983). Responsibility in the classroom: A synthesis of research on teaching self-control. *Educational Leadership, 40*(7), 62–66.

Baer, G. (1983). Discipline in the classroom: Perceptions of middle grade teachers. *Clearing House, 57,* 139–142.

Baker, J. (1985). Research evidence of a school discipline problem. *Phi Delta Kappan, 66,* 482–487.

Batesky, J. A. (1986). Twelve tips for better discipline, *Contemporary Education, 57,* 98–99.

Boynton, P. (1985). A basic survival guide for new teachers. *Clearing House, 59,* 101–103.

Canter, L. (1976). *Assertive discipline.* Los Angeles: Canter and Associates.

Clay, G. V. (1984). Maintaining order and discipline: A duty requiring knowledge of the law. *High School Journal, 67,* 178–184.

Ernst, K. (1985). *Games students play.* Millbrae CA: Celestial Arts.

Holmes, J. H. (1985). We can teach students to be responsible. *Phi Delta Kappan, 66,* 50–52.

McDaniel, T. R. (1986). A primer on classroom discipline: Principles old and new. *Phi Delta Kappan, 68,* 63–67.

Schmidt, F., & Friedman, A. (1987). Strategies for resolving classroom conflicts. *Learning, 15(6),* 40–42.

Schonberger, V. L. (1986). Effective discipline: A positive approach to self-direction and personal growth. *Contemporary Education, 58,* 30–34.

Shrigley, R. L. (1986). Teacher authority in the classroom: A plan for action. *NASSP Bulletin, 70,* 65–71.

Walsh, K. (1986). Classroom rights and discipline: A simple and effective system. *Learning, 14(7),* 66–67.

CASE 11

The Missing Ingredient: Can Excessive Planning Produce Rigidity?

Jean McCarthy was excited as she drove to Woodrow Wilson High School for her first week of student teaching. She was pleased to receive this particular assignment, not because of the particular school and, for certain, not because of its location. Woodrow Wilson High stands in the middle of a large ghetto. Jean's pleasure over this placement can be attributed to the school's home economics teacher, Margaret Hayes. In spite of the bleak surroundings, Ms. Hayes has earned a reputation for maintaining a permanent positive attitude toward her students, her job, and life itself.

Jean's secure feeling came to a standstill when after only three days Ms. Hayes contracted a virus and asked Jean to take over all five of her home economics classes. But Jean was a thorough planner and the first three sections went very smoothly. The fourth period was underway, and when it was over, the morning could soon be declared a success.

The day's lesson involved baking a batch of very simple cookies. All students watched attentively as she demonstrated. As this experimental batch reached a desired brown glow, Jean carefully removed them from the oven. When she set the hot pan of cookies on the butcher's block, she noticed that the bag of brown sugar that she had brought especially for this activity was unopened. Jean felt a chill of fear as she realized that she had forgotton to include perhaps the most important ingredient in any cookies—sugar. And she had planned to have the students sample them. Quickly, she wondered how to handle this situation. After all, she *is* the teacher, and the teacher shouldn't make such mistakes. She had planned a student critique of her work as each student sampled a cookie. Now they were ruined. And it was almost time to begin cleaning up in preparation for the next class. There was not enough time left in the period to bake another batch.

Immediately, Jean explained to the class what had happened. She then introduced the major concepts in the lesson, "texture" and "taste." But she altered the original intent, which was for the students to *develop the proper techniques* for attaining correct texture and taste. Now she emphasized *the importance* of texture and taste in cooking. She ended the lesson by having each student sample a cookie and describe both its texture and its taste. A good discussion was conducted as the students sampled the goods. Jean raised further questions such as, "How to do you think the texture and taste would be altered if we used unrefined sugar? How would these characteristics be affected if other ingredients were omitted? What additional ingredients could be added to improve the texture? Could the texture be improved while worsening the taste, and vice-versa?" The students enjoyed the latitude provided by these open-ended, divergent-type questions. Realizing her omission, Jean chose these types of questions because they stimulate students to be creative. Each time a student hesitated or provided an incorrect response, Jean provided hints that led the student to make correct responses.

As the lesson ended, Jean looked around to see the principal, Ms. Chissom, standing at the door. She had dropped by to see how things were going. All seemed well, but then Mrs. Chissom stared grimly at Jean and demanded to see her lesson plan, which Jean clearly had not followed. Or had she?

Upon examining the lesson plan, Ms. Chissom quickly realized that Jean had strayed from her original plan. In a private meeting with Jean later that afternoon, Ms. Chissom shared some of her concerns with Jean.

"First, I noticed that your summary was not a summary of the planned lesson at all. Do you think a teacher is ever justified in switching to a different lesson? Might this confuse students?"

Before Jean could respond to this concern, Ms. Chissom continued. "Secondly, our intent is to teach content and skills, yet I heard you asking divergent and opinion-seeking questions. We must teach our students that there is more to knowing home economics than opinion. Home economics is a science. Our cooking succeeds, when it succeeds at all, because of the laws of science and because we are skilled in the use of these laws. We shouldn't care so much about students' opinions as about their knowledge."

By this time, Jean could no longer contain herself. "Ms. Chissom, I puposefully asked open-ended, opinion-seeking questions because I want my students to be creative."

But obviously the day had been a long one for Ms. Chissom, who refused to listen to Jean. "It *has* been a long day. I will discuss this matter with you again during your planning period tomorrow."

With these words, Ms. Chissom left the room. Jean wondered how she should conduct her part of the discussion tomorrow.

THE CHALLENGE: Suppose you were in Jean's position. What would you do? Before deciding on a course of action, consider the following:

- This lesson was designed around a few important concepts that included techniques for improving texture and taste.
- The result of the lesson was the development of two similar, yet different, concepts—the *importance* of texture and taste.
- Jean did not attempt to cover up her mistake.
- Students were involved in the questioning session.
- The types of questions asked included divergent questions.

KEY ISSUES FOR STUDY:

1. Should teachers always be so honest with students?
2. Should all lessons be constructed around a few major concepts?
3. Was the teacher wrong in straying from the original lesson?
4. Is it wise to involve students during the lesson as these students were involved through testing these cookies?
5. Is inquiry learning an appropriate method for all subjects?
6. Should teachers attempt to involve students in every lesson?
7. What might be the results if a supervisor saw a beginning teacher "using" mistakes to teach?
8. Does a principal have a right to insist on seeing a teacher's lesson plan?
9. This teacher saw an opportunity to use her inquiry skills to turn a potentially disastrous lesson into a rich learning experience. Should teachers purposefully plan inquiry lessons to have students explore their subjects?
10. Teachers are frequently reminded of the need to cover all of their subject content so that their students will be prepared for next year; yet the inquiry approach is a very inefficient and slow method. Is it realistic to think that teachers really have time to use the inquiry method?

SUGGESTED READINGS

Hamm, R. L. (1985). Teaching as learning. *Contemporary Education, 56,* 201.

Smith, L. J., & Smith, D. L. (1986). Experiential learning: Teaching teachers to transfer their knowledge. *Journal of Reading, 29,* 342–345.

Smith, L. R. (1985). The effect of lesson structure and cognitive level of questions on student achievement. *The Journal of Experimental Education, 54,* 44–49.

Specht, P. H. (1985). Experiential learning-based vs. lecture-based discussion: The impact of degree of participation and student characteristics on comprehension and retention. *Journal of Business Education, 60,* 283–287.

Sugarman, L. (1985). Kolb's model of experiential learning: Touchstone for trainers, students, counselors, and clients. *Journal of Counseling Development, 64*, 264–268.

Wilson, B. G. (1985). Using content structure in course design. *Journal of Educational Technology Systems, 14*(2), 137–147.

CASE 12

Multicultural Education and the Challenge of Self-image

Andrew Jackson Elementary School is located in a major city in the midwest. Once known as the most innovative school in this large urban system, a changing neighborhood has altered significantly the priorities of the school. No longer are time and money directed to experimental teaching and curriculum development; rather, resources are focused upon serving the needs of children from low-income families. The neighborhood was once a thriving area, but the closing of two steel mills caused untold miseries for its residents. Many of the adults held semiskilled jobs in the mills, and finding new employment has been extremely difficult. Increasingly, families who could afford to leave the area have done so.

The current enrollment of the school is listed as 80 percent black, 18 percent white, and 2 percent other. The faculty, on the other hand, is 75 percent white and 25 percent black. The principal, Margaret Dickerson, is black, and she has been at the school only one year. A number of the more experienced teachers at Jackson Elementary have lived through the transition of the past twenty years. Thus, some of the most respected elementary school teachers in the system continue to teach at Jackson.

Janice Nichols is a first-year teacher assigned to teach second grade at the school. Janice is the daughter of Drs. William and Nadine Nichols. Her father is a professor of microbiology and her mother is a psychiatrist. Janice is black. A graduate of a prestigious university, she chose to be a teacher and to work in an inner-city environment. Neither of her parents was thrilled by her career decision, but both admired her dedication to working with underprivileged children.

Janice's class at Jackson is rather typical for the school. The class consists mostly of black children; about one-fourth are white. Virtually all of the students come from families that have below-average incomes or are at the poverty-level. One of the students in Janice's classroom, Maria, identifies with neither the black nor the white students. Maria's parents recently rented an apartment in the Jackson school district. They are from Puerto Rico and have been on the mainland for only seven months. Although at times Maria exhibits signs of being very bright, she is withdrawn and avoids social contact with the other children. For Janice, Maria has become a very special challenge. There is little doubt in Janice's mind that Maria's behavior is inhibiting her academic progress.

After three months of unsuccessful attempts to engage Maria more fully in classroom activities, Janice requested that the parents come in for a conference. Maria's mother agreed to come to school, but the encounter proved to be of little value. The mother spoke little English and simply nodded and smiled in response to everything Janice said. In frustration, Janice took the problem to Mrs. Dickerson, the principal. Mrs. Dickerson suggested an examination by the school psychologist and Janice proceeded to make the arrangements.

Two weeks after the scheduled examination of Maria, Janice received the following report:

> Results of Examination:
>
> Maria exhibits above-average intelligence. Her verbal skills are not an accurate measure of her ability. She comes from a home environment where English is rarely used as a means of communication. Much of Maria's language ability comes from watching television and listening to peers in school. She has two siblings—a brother who is three years old and a sister who is one year old. No problems were identified with either auditory or visual perceptions.
>
> The child appears to have a serious self-image problem. This is probably due to the lack of other Hispanic children in the educational environment. Maria admitted during the examination that both black and white children have told her that she is "different." She is unable to verbalize what this means; but obviously this peer judgment has had a negative effect upon her adjustment to this school's environment. Attention should be given to infusing multicultural education into the classroom activities. Directed interaction with select students should be a high priority.
>
> Arnold Davis, Ph.D.
School Psychologist

Upon reading the report, Janice's first course of action was to see Mrs. Dickerson. The principal acknowledged that she had read the psychologist's report and agreed with it. Janice said, "What I really need is some help. I'm not sure how I can implement the recommendations the psychologist made."

"Well," responded Mrs. Dickerson, "I'm not sure how you should proceed with this either. Give it some thought and see what resources you can find to help you. In any event, we need to come up with a positive course of action."

THE CHALLENGE: You must assume Janice's role. How would you deal with this issue?

KEY ISSUES FOR STUDY:

1. List potential resources in the school that might help you address this need.
2. List potential resources outside the school that might help you address this need.
3. Do you think that Principal Dickerson was meeting her responsibilities in this matter? Why or why not?
4. List additional information regarding this entire issue that might help you decide upon a course of action.
5. Identify the data in the case that are most relevant to addressing the needs of Maria. Identify data that are not relevant.
6. Identify ways in which multicultural education could be used to address Maria's needs.
7. As a result of the psychologist's report, what goals would you establish: (a) with regard to Maria, (b) with regard to the remainder of the class?
8. Maria's problem presents an opportunity for you to help her classmates develop social responsibility. How might you approach these students to entice them to invite Maria and other minority students to join their activities?

SUGGESTED READINGS

Bishop, G. R. (1986). The identification of multicultural materials for the middle school library: Annotations and sources. *American Middle School Education*, *9*, 23–27.

Brady, M. (1984). Understanding the minority child in the American educational system. *Education*, *105*(1), 21–33.

Cheyney, A. B. (1976). Teaching children of different cultures in the classroom (2nd ed.). Columbus, OH: Charles E. Merrill.

DeCosta, S. (1984). Not all children are Anglo and middle class: A practical beginning for the elementary teacher. *Theory into Practice*, *23*, 155–162.

Henson, K. (1987). Teaching in multicultural settings. *In Methods and strategies for teaching in secondary and middle schools* (pp. 199–219). White Plains, NY: Longman.

Wardle, F. (1987). Are you sensitive to interracial children's special identity needs? *Young Child*, *42*(2), 53–59.

Wieseman, R. (1986). Multicultural beginnings and early learning. *Journal of Instructional Psychology*, *13*, 172–176.

Cheating—A Problem for All

THE COMMUNITY

Horton, a small, rural community, is unincorporated and therefore has no distinct boundaries. The population is about two hundred. Most of the neighboring communities are no larger; some are smaller and some have such names as Needmore, Bean Blossom, Sneeds Crossroads, and Reform. The major industry is pulpwood. Most communities have sprung up from logging camps. The population is highly conservative. Most residents belong to either the local Baptist or Methodist church. Several families attend the primitive Baptist church, which does not believe in Sunday school or musical instruments. The little gas station has a bench out front where a few of the senior residents spend time playing checkers and discussing the crops, the weather, and the high school basketball games.

The pick-up truck is still the most popular mode of transportation in the region. Most are equipped with gun racks and either Copenhagen or Skoal tool chests. Visitors often complain that these vehicles usually travel down the center of the narrow farm-to-market roads. The oversize tires offer an additional threat.

THE SCHOOL AND ITS LEADERSHIP

Pine Grove Elementary School reminds most visitors of a turn-of-the-century school. Each of its six rooms accommodates a grade level. The principal, Ms. Janice Blackwood, teaches two periods each day. This keeps her abreast of teaching and its new developments and challenges, and it makes both the students and teachers at Pine Grove Elementary respect the fact that she understands the perspectives of both teachers and students. Her pragmatic philosophy seems to fit this locale. She endorses the concept of experiential education and encourages the other teachers to combine direct instruction coupled with hands-on experiences. Her hands-on approach is appreciated by the rugged, work-oriented parents. Ms. Blackwood has provided strong leadership for the school for the past fifteen years. To the residents, who respect her understanding but no-nonsense approach, she symbolizes Pine Grove. The students and teachers consider her firm, yet fair.

On one occasion, which involved two students changing their grades in their teacher's grade book, Ms. Blackwood arranged a meeting with the students and their parents. She firmly assured them that any recurrence of the problem would find the students giving a public apology in their classes and that a note of their dishonest behavior would be placed in their cumulative files. Needless to say, there were no further instances of this behavior. The incident led to the development of a policy statement on cheating.

THE TEACHER

Hans Anderson taught his first two years in a large urban school. He moved to this community a year ago because he wanted to live in the mountains. The serenity and the natural setting have been all he had hoped for. The residents seem to have an unwritten code of acceptance. His love for the outdoors provides excellent opportunities for Hans to get close to his sixth-grade students. Saturdays are often spent with some of his students hunting or fishing. As part of a unit on plants, he takes nature hikes with some of the less sporting students. His students enjoy competing with each other as they use a key that he provides them to classify trees. They enjoy similar experiences when studying a unit on rocks and minerals, using outdoor hikes to collect specimens and fossils and sedimentary, igneous, and metamorphic rocks. They frequently visit a chirt pit, which the county road commissioner had dug to provide rocks for road beds, but which Hans and his students use to collect crinoid stems. Some have even found some petrified flowers and round bulbs that anchored the crinoid plants. Most of the students show their appreciation by applying their efforts on classroom and homework assignments. The first year has proven that Hans has found a permanent home.

THE INCIDENT

For Hans's classes, Friday is known as test day. Today was no different. As Hans often kidded, "Friday is our sharing day; it's the day that I give you the opportunity to share some of your knowledge with me." At the beginning of each test period, Hans introduces a little levity to lower the anxiety. It is clearly understood that once the test is underway, there is to be no foolishness. Unlike some teachers who use test periods to catch up on their paperwork or to stand in their doorway and chat with their neighboring teachers, Hans never leaves the room during a test; in fact, he seldom uses test time to grade papers, fill out the monthly report, or perform other chores. Instead, Hans is determined to give his full attention to monitoring the test.

This Friday was typical in that once the test was underway a silence fell across the class. Hans sat positioned in front of the room staring directly at the students in his sixth-grade classes as they steadily worked through the test. He was stunned to see one of his students, Sharon King, looking directly at her neighbor's paper, which was only partially covered, as her classmate Bobby Stephens worked attentively on the test. Hans's first thoughts were that this can't be happening. Sharon continued to stare openly at the uncovered test. She didn't write while she stared, nor did she ever look forward to see whether she was being watched. Equally puzzling was the fact that Hans's students had repeatedly been told that anyone who is ever careless enough to leave a test exposed is guilty of contributing to the cheating. In his own words, "Those who let others copy their tests or homework are just as guilty as those who copy." Bobby Stephens was not the type of student who would deliberately help a classmate cheat. In fact, Bobby was so competitive that he would be more likely to go to great lengths to keep his competition "in check." In school policy it is written that when teachers catch students cheating the teacher will administer "appropriate" punishment, but it does not define *appropriate*.

Hans wondered whether it was possible that Sharon could be unaware that she was looking directly at her classmate's paper. Perhaps she was daydreaming; that wasn't unusual for Sharon—but during a test? It didn't make sense. Hans had not taken his eyes off of Sharon. The other students were so busy taking the test that it was unlikely that any of them had noticed.

THE DECISION

Hans considered what he should do. He had heard of teachers taking test papers away from students who cheated and throwing the tests in the wastebasket. This seemed a little harsh. For many students, receiving a zero on a weekly test would result in failure of the six-week period. Hans wondered whether this were the case with Sharon and whether he should check her six-week average before making a decision. He also thought about what he should do to Sharon's neighbor.

THE CHALLENGE: Cheating is a concern of all teachers. Suppose you were in Hans's predicament. What would you do? Before responding, consider the following:

- Pine Grove Elementary School is located in a rural conservative community.
- The principal, Ms. Blackwood is a strong, respected leader.
- Ms. Blackwood supports Hans's experiential approach to education.
- Hans Anderson enjoys teaching and he even gives much of his weekends to fishing, hunting, and hiking with his students.
- Hans carefully monitors students as they take his tests.
- Hans has discussed the seriousness of copying information during tests.
- Hans has also discussed the responsibility that all students have to keep their test answers covered at all times.
- Both Bobby and Sharon had earned reputations of being honest and trustworthy.
- Most Horton community residents express their religious convictions through attending church services regularly.
- Ms. Blackwood, the principal, has taken a firm stand against cheating.
- Neither Bobby nor Sharon gave the impression that they were sneaking the transfer of information. On the contrary, both seemed unaware that cheating was going on.
- Hans has established a routine of giving weekly tests. Could this make students more sensitive to the seriousness of test taking? Less sensitive?

KEY ISSUES FOR STUDY:

1. When dealing with a problem of cheating, should a student's prior academic performance be considered?
2. List several alternative behaviors that Hans could take. (Hint: Choosing to do nothing is itself an alternative.)
3. Rank-order the behaviors listed in response to question 2.
4. For each alternative, tell what additional information is needed, if any.
5. Explain how each alternative would affect Sharon's relationship with her teacher.
6. Explain how each alternative might change other classmates' perception of their teacher.
7. Divide your list of alternatives into immediate behaviors and long-term behaviors.
8. What kind of penalties are needed to assure that students do not make their work available to others?
9. In what ways do community values affect your decision?
10. Why do some teachers give tests at definite intervals? How does this routine approach affect the degree of seriousness that students feel toward tests?

SUGGESTED READINGS

Aspy, D. N. (1986). Fulfilling the great tradition through interpersonal honesty: A response to Wynne. *Educational Leadership*, *43*, 13–14.

Burton, R. V. (1981). Can ethics be taught? *New York University Education Quarterly*, *12*, 29–32.

Casey, W. M., & Burton, R. V. (1983). Training children to be honest through verbal self-instruction. *Child Development*, *53*, 911–919.

Cook, J., & Gracenin, C. (1981). When is copying cheating? *Early Years*, *12*, 29–32.

Fowler, D. H. (1986). Cheating: A bigger problem than meets the eye. *NASSP Bulletin*, *70*, 93–96.

Houser, B. B. (1982). Student cheating and attitude: A function of classroom teachnique. *Contemporary Educational Psychology*, *7*, 113–123.

Keane, B. M. (1984). Are you modeling honesty in your high school classroom? *Momentum*, *15*, 36–38.

McBryde, N. M. (1987). Realities of cheating: Preventing, not cures. *American Secondary Education*, *15*(4), 19–20.

Miller, H. L. (1986). The fine line between cheating and helping. *Early Years*, *17*, 104–105.

Morris, C. W. Abscam in the classroom, or lessons from Washington. *English Journal*, *71*, 40–41.

Newhouse, R. C. (1982). Alienation and cheating behavior in the school environment. *Psychology in the Schools*, *19*, 234–237.

Schab, F. (1980). Cheating in high school: Differences among the sexes. *Adolescence*, *15*, 959–965.

Stevens, G. E. (1984). Ethical inclination of tomorrow's citizens: Actions speak louder? *Journal of Business Education*, *59*, 147–152.

CASE 14

Spare the Rod and Spoil the Teacher?

THE COMMUNITY

Johnson Falls is a relatively small city exhibiting remarkable growth. Recently, a major Japanese manufacturing company decided to build a new electronics plant in the community. This is the third new industry to locate in Johnson Falls since an industrial park was developed six years ago. The current population of 17,300 is nearly double what it was ten years ago.

Mayor Jane Anderson is fond of saying that her city is the model for the state and the entire southwestern part of the country. She points to the increase in population, relatively low cost of housing and land, access to a state university in the community, bountiful natural resources, and an outstanding local school system. Just four months ago, one of the national television networks did a special on Johnson Falls, tabbing it the "American city on the move."

But growth has its costs. Taxes, especially for schools and city services, have increased nearly 35 percent in the last five years. Virtually all of the new residents are transplants from the midwest and the northeast. Some are professionals employed by Johnson Falls State University (an institution that has grown from 2,000 students to 7,000 students in the last decade); some are managerial personnel employed by the expanding industries; but most are factory workers seeking a better life in the southwest.

For many of the natives of Johnson Falls, growth has been bitter sweet. Landowners, for example, have profited significantly as new subdivisions and retail businesses have been developed. Yet the benefits of economic prosperity are diminished by the realization that the new residents bring with them different values, beliefs, and priorities.

Mayor Anderson is one of the few leaders trusted by new and old residents alike. The daughter of the founder of the bank in Johnson Falls, she advocates compromise and understanding. She is devoted to bridging the differences that exist between the community's two elements.

THE SCHOOL SYSTEM

Johnson Falls Community School District has struggled to serve the growing educational needs of the community. Just seven years ago the school system consisted of a junior/senior high school and two elementary schools. Now there is a new high school, a middle school (housed in the former junior/senior high), and five elementary schools.

The hiring of Superintendent John Burdlow two years ago serves as an excellent example of how differing values in the community are surfacing. The composition of the school board, consisting of seven members elected at-large, changed dramatically after an election three years ago. A slate of three candidates, all of whom had lived in the community less than two years, was elected. They united politically with a dissident already on the board and their first act of defiance was to dismiss the superintendent who had served in that role for eighteen years. To make matters worse, that superintendent was a lifelong resident of the community. After that action, they employed Dr. Burdlow, a New Yorker who had never set foot in Johnson Falls before his interview.

At the same time that a new element was elected to the school board, Mayor Anderson assumed the post of mayor. She has worked closely with Superintendent Burdlow to make the schools an asset rather than a source of conflict. It was at her urging, for example, that several professors from the local university were brought in to work with staff to understand the changing social dynamics of Johnson Falls.

THE SCHOOL

Northside Elementary School is the oldest of the five elementary schools in the district. Located in the established part of town, the school has two sections per grade level. Principal Nancy Turkel is in her eleventh year as administrator of the school. She has been in the school system since graduating from Johnson Falls State University nineteen years ago.

Not serving the growth areas of Johnson Falls, Northside Elementary has been less burdened with conflict than have the other schools. The teaching staff has the highest average age of any of the schools in the system, and many of them, like Principal Turkel, are "locals" who graduated from Johnson Falls State University.

THE TEACHER

Carol Deangelo is the only first-year teacher at Northside Elementary. In fact, she is the only new teacher to be hired at this school in several years. A graduate of a private college in the northeast, Carol was thrilled to get a teaching position when her husband, Tom, was transferred to Johnson Falls by his employer. She was an above-average student in college who did not decide to become a teacher until after her sophomore year.

Carol's assignment is fourth grade. She has a class of twenty-seven students. The first two months of school have been challenging, but enjoyable. Carol has not established any close relationships with other teachers; but given that they are all much older, she has not been especially troubled by this. Principal Turkel has been helpful and supportive.

THE INCIDENT

Both fourth-grade classes were together in the gymnasium to view a science film. Carol operated the projector while Margie Stowe, the other teacher, walked slowly about the room searching for signs of misbehavior. Mrs. Stowe is an authority figure in the school. The other teachers admire her for her willingness to confront difficult issues. Even the principal is respectful of her powers of persuasion.

About midway through the film, Mrs. Stowe yelled, "Stop the projector!" Pointing at two boys in Carol's class, she shouted, "Okay, you two get out in the hall right now!"

"What happened?" Carol asked.

"Those two have been punching each other ever since we started. They need to be taught a lesson," Mrs. Stowe exclaimed.

Mrs. Stowe turned to the other students. "You be quiet. Mrs. Deangelo and I have to deal with these two rowdies. I don't want to hear a peep until we get back."

With that she turned and headed for the hallway, motioning Carol to follow. As they reached the hallway door, she stopped and said, "Go to your room and get your paddle. These two have to be taught a lesson. If you don't discipline them right now, word will spread among the students that they can get by with this behavior in your class. If there is one thing I can tell you from all my years of experience, it's that you have to be a firm disciplinarian to survive."

"But I don't even have a paddle," Carol responded.

"Well I do, and you can use mine."

"Isn't paddling students against the school policies?" Carol asked.

"Who knows. This new school board is changing things so rapidly—who can keep up? I'll tell you this, at Northside we still believe that a good paddling is something most of these kids understand."

"What about Mrs. Turkel? Doesn't she say anything about breaking school district policies?"

Mrs. Stowe stared at Carol and said, "She doesn't ask and we don't say anything. The parents support what we do. I have never had a parent argue that I shouldn't discipline a child. In fact, many of the kids know that if their parents find out that they were paddled at school, they would get another paddling at home. Now are you going to paddle these boys or am I going to have to do your work for you?"

THE CHALLENGE: Put yourself in Carol's position. What would you do?

KEY ISSUES FOR STUDY:

1. Does paddling or other forms of corporal punishment deter undesirable behavior? Explain your answer.
2. What risks does Carol take if she decides to paddle the two boys?
3. What risks does Carol take if she decides not to paddle the two boys?
4. If Carol permits Mrs. Stowe to paddle these students, how will Carol's relation- ship with them and the other students in this class be affected?
5. Is it legal for a teacher to administer corporal punishment? Explain your answer.
6. To what degree are environmental (the community) and organizational (the school district and school) conditions responsible for the situation Carol faces?
7. Where could Carol turn for help in this matter?
8. Is there some way that Carol could prevent Mrs. Stowe from paddling the students? Explain your answer.
9. Is Mrs. Stowe correct in her judgment that failure to paddle the boys will be viewed as a sign of weakness by the other students in Carol's class? Explain your answer.
10. To what degree would you permit your own values and beliefs to govern your behavior in this situation?
11. What additional information would you like to have in deciding how to respond in this situation?
12. If a state permits corporal punishment, may a school district through policy prohibit its use?

SUGGESTED READINGS

Curwin, R., & Mendler, A. (1988). *Discipline with dignity*. Alexandria, VA: Associa- tion for Supervision and Curriculum Development.

Henderson, D. (1986). Constitutional implications involving the use of corporal punishment in the public schools: A comprehensive review. *Journal of Law and Education, 15,* 255–269.

Henson, K. T. (1986). Corporal punishment: Ten popular myths. *The High School Journal, 69*(2), 107–109.

Kessler, G. (1985). Spanking in school: Deterrent or barbarism? *Childhood Education*, *61*, 175–176.

Nolte, M. C. (1985). Before you take a paddling in court, read this corporal punishment advice. *American School Board Journal*, *173*(7), 27, 35.

Tuhus, M. (1987). It's time we stop paddling kids. *Instructor*, *96*(7), 16–19.

Zirkel, P., & Reichner, H. (1987). Is "in loco parentis" dead? *Phi Delta Kappan*, *68*, 466–469.

CASE 15

From Eagles to Crows—
The Impact of Ability Grouping

"I've found the neatest stickers for my reading and math groups," Ginger Halcom began, as she pulled samples from her purse. "Look. Bluebirds for the middle group, Eagles for the high-flyers. And crows for the slow learners."

"Those are prettier than your old ones. And fuzzy," Bryan King observed, as he examined the stickers.

"You aren't really going to use those, are you?" Celeste Mecham inquired.

"Of course I am," Ginger responded, somewhat indignantly. "I've used stickers every year of the fourteen I've taught."

"I do too," Bryan King agreed. "except I like to use flowers—roses for the brightest children, violets for the middle group, and daisies for the slowest."

"Don't the children feel funny being identified that way?" Celeste Mecham asked.

"No," the other two teachers replied in unison.

"They love it," Ginger chided.

"It helps them identify. Know where they stand," Bryan King added.

The bell rang, ending the lunch period. The three teachers returned to their classrooms. The teachers have twenty-eight children in their self-contained classrooms. The children reflect a social and intellectual balance—a wide range of academic abilities and economic backgrounds.

Celeste Mecham was in her third week at Comstock Elementary. Each week she had become more distressed by the behavior of her planning team members—an instructional planning group implemented in her school by the principal. The lunchtime conversation added to her anger. From the first time the team met she had felt at odds. Initially, she thought it was probably due to age and teaching experience.

Together, Ginger Halcom and Bryan King represent a half-century of classroom practice. They are alike in many ways. Both are single, claiming to have devoted their lives to teaching. Both are hard-working teachers who care deeply about their students, and both are graduates of an eastern liberal arts college. They share an emphasis on reading, writing, and arithmetic. They believe that the development of the mind is the primary, overriding purpose of teaching. The development of most other goals, they agree, is better left to parents. They share the view that children should be taught at their level of ability.

In some respects, they differ. Mr. King has been teaching for three more years; he specialized in science and mathematics; he enjoys traveling, and lists gourmet cooking and playing the piano as hobbies. In contrast, Ms. Halcom is a member of the Daughters of the American Revolution and relishes history. She is an avid reader, appreciates art, and rarely travels. She has never ventured beyond 127 miles from her birthplace.

Ms. Mecham is a neophyte, beginning her first year. A graduate of a top-rated teacher training institution in the midwest, she feels well prepared for her first job. She had participated in a special undergraduate program that doubled the number of field experiences she had and integrated the disciplines in organized blocks of time. During her junior year she spent a semester abroad, working in a British infant school. She feels well grounded in recent research on effective teaching. Creativity and a mature understanding of instructional theory and its application to practice are strengths in her training.

On nearly every issue she and the two veterans disagreed. The most serious disagreement among the team members began before the start of the school year. During the two workdays before classes began, the three team members shared information on the children they would be teaching. Mr. King talked about the children he had had in first grade the year before who were now assigned to Ms. Mecham's second-grade class. Because Ms. Mecham was new, he also told Ms. Halcom what he knew about the third-graders he had had in class two years before. More than half of one day was devoted to sharing stories about the children and their families, and assigning the youngsters to reading and mathematics groups. For the new children in the classes, the teachers examined and discussed "criterion-referenced" tests traditionally used in the school for diagnosing ability levels.

Ms. Mecham was shocked by the personal matters the teachers discussed. She was equally uncomfortable making assignments without knowing the children. Based on her studies in the teacher education program at City University, she had become suspicious of the value of ability grouping. At one point in the discussion she asked the teachers why they used ability grouping. The teachers responded with disdain. "It has always been done this way at Comstock," they said, "and it works!" She had felt devastated that they would not even listen to her views on the subject.

Reluctantly, she had implemented ability grouping in her second-grade classroom. For the most part, the same children were assigned to the low groups in both subjects. To her surprise, she found that ability grouping with the high-achieving groups in mathematics and reading had been somewhat successful. Individual progress had been more rapid than she had expected. She had been worried that her negative attitude toward ability grouping might prove to be a self-filling prophecy—that her students would not do well because of her attitude. Although achievement for the high-ability students had progressed favorably, she was bothered by some problems that had arisen.

On three occasions during the first two weeks, Celeste Mecham had to break up fights on the playground between children from the low-ability groups and the high-ability groups. In many cases children who worked together in the ability groups tended to congregate and play together during recess. In each of the fighting incidents, the source of conflict resulted from name-calling. The high-ability students tagged the slower children as "dummies." The low-ability children had retorted with "brats" and "weirdos." Celeste's lectures about cooperating and respecting differences had gone unheeded. Grouping children in other ways during other instructional activities and games had had little impact.

Ms. Mecham had become increasingly concerned about the low-ability children. Early in the year some of them had impressed her as energetic, thoughtful, and attentive. But once they had been labeled, they seemed to slip into a more passive, listless role. She noticed that they had become less willing to participate in activities, tended to make more errors, gave up sooner on tasks, and had become more attached to other members of their group. In the classroom, when asked to work with other children from middle and high-ability groups, they rebelled the loudest and strongest. Children in low-ability groups in both reading and mathematics behaved similarly.

During the afternoon she went through the motions of teaching, but her thoughts drifted back to the conversation in the faculty lounge. When she went home at the end of the day, Celeste Mecham still felt troubled and tried to call Dr. Marsha Wellington, a professor of elementary education at City University, who had been assigned by the university to work with Celeste as part of its teachers' induction program. Dr. Wellington had visited on the first day of class and had told Celeste to call her at work or at home if she needed to talk.

"I've got to get out of this mess," Celeste thought to herself. "I can't go on grouping these children this way. I don't believe in it, and I'm unhappy."

But there was no answer at Dr. Wellington's work or at home. "I don't know what I'm going to do. I can't stand another day," she muttered aloud.

THE CHALLENGE: You are Ms. Mecham. What will you do?

KEY ISSUES FOR STUDY:

1. What solution to Ms. Mecham's concerns about ability grouping would you propose?
2. What evidence from the case led you to this decision?
3. What are potential positive results of your decision?
4. What are potential negative consequences of your decision?
5. What additional information would you like before making a decision?
6. What information in this case is not relevant for making a decision?

SUGGESTED READINGS

Berliner, D. C. (1985). Does ability grouping cause more problems than it solves? *Instructor, 94,* 14–15.

Bloom, B. S. (1984). The search for methods of group instruction as effective as one-to-one tutoring. *Educational Leadership, 41*(8), 4–17.

Bracey, G. (1986). Ability grouping and student achievement in elementary schools. *Phi Delta Kappan, 68,* 76–77.

Cohen, P. A. & Kulik, J. (1981). Synthesis on research on the effects of tutoring. *Educational Leadership, 39*(3), 227–229.

Jongsma, E. (1985). Grouping for instruction. *Reading Teacher, 38*(9), 918–920.

Morehead, M., & Waters, S. (1985/86). Grouping students. *Teacher Educator, 21,* 29–32.

Moyer, J. (1986). Child development as a base for decision-making. *Childhood Education, 62,* 325–329.

Nevi, C. (1987). In defense of tracking. *Educational Leadership, 44,* 24–26.

Riccio, L. L. (1985). Facts and issues about ability grouping. *Contemporary Education, 57,* 26–30.

Schmida, M. (1987). Ability grouping and students' social orientation. *Urban Education, 21*(4), 421–431.

Slavin, R. E. (1980). Cooperative learning. *Review of Educational Research, 50*(2), 315–542.

Slavin, R. E. (1981). Synthesis of research on cooperative learning. *Educational Leadership 38*(8), 655–659.

CASE 16

Who Should Evaluate Teachers?

THE SCHOOL

Riverside Junior High School is a rural school bordered by the Brazos River, State Highway 30, and large open fields. Over the years, the overflow of the flooded river has deposited a dry layer of silt, making excellent top soil, rich in all types of minerals. Because of their love of the land the farmers who comprise most of the community residents are very stable. Generation after generation have remained on the farms.

The Riverside Junior High parking lot gives a visitor a clue as to the type of faculty who teach at this school. Most of the vehicles are pick-up trucks with scratches from running across the fields, pastures, and wooded areas. The beds shine where the paint has been worn off by animal hoofs. The sporty cars and the few shiny new, dressed-up trucks belong to some of the older ninth-grade students.

In one important respect the faculty inside resembles most faculties; it is made up of individuals, teachers of varying levels of ability and commitment.

Anyone who has had extensive experience working with teachers in their schools knows that each school has some highly competent teachers whose leadership emerges each time a job is to be done. For example, when it is time to prepare for a regional accreditation review, a small core of teachers stands ready to take charge. These teachers are highly competent, bright, and motivated. They thrive on challenges. They are the "doers."

Unfortunately, experienced educators know that most faculties also have a collection of teachers who are the opposite of the "doers." These teachers also stand ready, but not ready to get the job done; they stand ready to complain and to run away from new responsibilities. Most of them are equipped with a storehouse full of reasons why a new activity won't work, why it's a waste of time, and why it isn't good for the students, the school, or the country. Usually these teachers have practiced dodging responsibilities so much that they have developed a complete repertoire of evasion skills, which enable them to escape most responsibilities—thus rendering them harmless. Yet in rare instances where these skilled evaders get trapped into performing a task, conditions are ripe for the making of disasters. This case is about one of those disasters.

THE CONFLICT

Marge Stokes, a seventh-grade English teacher at Riverside Junior High, is a champion complainer, skilled in the art of escaping assignments. No one knows how she managed to be assigned a major role in Riverside's new career ladder program. Before Marge herself knew what had happened, she had been designated the language program supervisor, making her responsible for evaluating all English and speech teachers in grades seven through nine.

Marge's colleagues were as surprised as she was by her new role, for they had heard stories of Marge's own mediocre teaching. Some of the teachers thought the whole situation was quite comical, but these teachers did not teach English or speech. Those who taught English or speech knew that their future merit pay, advancement in the system, and professional reputations all rested on Marge's evaluations, and they didn't see one bit of humor in what they considered to be a travesty of justice.

In respect for her feelings, these teachers were reluctant to complain about the school's choice of this new supervisor. Yet underneath, Marge's colleagues felt that they had already been victimized by the principal's cavalier selection of Marge. A heated controversy had already developed in response to the emergence of the career ladder plan. Many teachers had said that they considered career ladders unprofessional because they label a few teachers "master teachers," thus implying that all other teachers are something less. Some said that subjecting teachers to evaluations by their peers is humiliating and unprofessional. Others went so far as to call this practice immoral.

At first, Marge was chagrined by having been caught and given an assignment. But as she began visiting classrooms to critique and evaluate teachers, Marge began to sense a feeling of power and status inherent in her new role. To put it bluntly, the new assignment went to her head. Her attitude was expressed in her often unkind, condescending remarks about her colleagues' performance. She promptly had some large, eight-inch rubber stamps made to mark the teachers' lesson plans. Each stamp had its own colored ink pad.

The stamps incensed the English and speech faculty members. A large blue stamp said UNACCEPTABLE; a black stamp said REJECTED; a red stamp said REDO; and a green stamp said DO OVER. She had no signs that signified approval. In conversations in the lounge, the faculty agreed that the situation was unacceptable and was deteriorating daily. What should they do? What *could* they do?

THE CHALLENGE: Suppose you were an English teacher at Riverside Junior High. How would you respond to Marge's requests? First, consider that

- Marge has a reputation for being a mediocre teacher.
- Marge is a complainer.
- Marge's appointment was a unilateral administrative decision; faculty input was not sought.
- The English and speech teachers were outraged by her appointment.
- Marge enjoyed the power and status of her role.
- Frequently, Marge's behavior reflected a superior attitude toward her colleagues.

KEY ISSUES FOR STUDY:

1. Should teachers be forced by state education department or districtwide mandates to have career ladders?
2. What advantages do career ladders offer teachers? Students?
3. Should teachers be evaluated by their colleagues? Why or why not?
4. Can school administrators legally force a career ladder on their faculty?
5. How should supervisors or evaluators of teachers be selected?
6. Is there evidence indicating that the selection of Marge for this role was a good choice?
7. How does peer evaluation affect the level of prestige of teaching? Can you name other professions that are regulated by peer evaluation? What advantages does this offer to teachers?
8. Does Marge have qualities that would make her a bad choice for this evaluation role? A good choice?

SUGGESTED READINGS

Darling-Hammond, L. (1986). Teacher evaluation: A proposal. *Education Digest, 52,* 30–33.

Edwards, C. M. (1986). Our performance pay gives teachers an incentive to improve. *American School Board Journal, 173,* 48–49.

Kauchak, S. (1985). An interview study of teachers' attitudes toward teacher evaluation practices. *Journal of Research and Development in Education, 19,* 32–37.

Kuzsman, F. J., & Harte, A. (1985). Teacher supervision and classroom improvement. *Education Digest*, *51*, 30–31.

Laing, S. O. (1986). The principal and evaluation. *NASSP Bulletin*, *70*, 91–93.

McCormick, K. (1985). Use peer review or something else, but act to end classroom incompetence. *American School Board Journal*, *172*, 23–24.

Sportsman, M. A. (1986). Evaluating teachers' performance fairly. *Curriculum Review*, *25*, 8–10.

Turner, R. R. (1986). Teachers speak about their evaluations. *Learning*, *15(2)*, 58–60.

Turner, R. R. (1987). What teachers think about their evaluations. *Education Digest*, *52*, 40–43.

CASE 17

Let's Get Tough— Assign More Homework

Midville is a quiet community of 13,000 people in a north-central state. The major industry in the town is a corn-processing plant owned by a large midwest company. The town has a hospital and serves as the county seat of Carroll County. In recent years the population has been declining and the local Chamber of Commerce has launched a campaign to attract new industry. The public schools have been asked to cooperate in a growth plan for the community.

The public school system includes a high school, a middle school, and four elementary schools. A year ago the board of education dismissed the superintendent who had been in that position for seventeen years. Citing a need for higher standards and higher expectations, the board employed Dr. John Rogers as its new superintendent. Dr. Rogers has embarked on a campaign to improve the image of the school system. During the past year he dismissed the high school principal and promised to do the same with remaining principals if positive change was not accomplished.

Mitchell West was unaware of this turmoil when he accepted a teaching position in Midville five months earlier. Having graduated from a state university in a neighboring state, he was thankful to get a job in a relatively small, peaceful community. He did not want to work in either an urban or suburban setting. Mitchell was assigned to teach fifth grade at Central Elementary School, a kindergarten through grade five school enrolling 320 pupils. The other fifth-grade teacher at Central Elementary is Elaine O'Rourke, a veteran of twenty-seven years of teaching in Midville.

The year had started off quite well for Mitchell. Everyone, including his principal, Susan Jones, was helpful and friendly. Mitchell was influenced heavily by his belief that school ought to be a place where students enjoy themselves. He was convinced that happy students work harder and make more progress than do those who dislike school. Thus, Mitchell made a concerted effort to make his classroom a pleasurable environment.

The students like Mitchell—perhaps too much. Principal Jones has had two letters recently from parents requesting that their children be transferred from Miss O'Rourke's class to Mr. West's class. Although the requests were denied, Miss O'Rourke managed to find out about the letters and was infuriated that the parents even initiated such action. Her displeasure prompted her to write a letter to Principal Jones stating her feelings:

Dear Mrs. Jones:

The requests to remove two students from my classroom are quite disturbing. I hope you take the time to probe into the "real" reasons why the parents wanted this done. I have nothing against Mr. West. With time, he will probably become a good teacher. However, he seems to have the idea that being popular is more important than being effective. Teaching is not a popularity contest. If Mr. West demanded from his students what I demand from mine, this situation would not have occurred.

Dr. Rogers has emphasized quality education in our school system. I totally support his effort to get rid of the "dead weight" around here. Part of achieving excellence is expecting more from our children. Mr. West rarely gives homework. He rarely punishes students. He often acts more like a big brother than a teacher. Normally I would not speak out; but I fear my reputation is damaged when parents ask to have their children removed from my class. I trust you will take action to see that this problem is addressed.

Thank you.
Sincerely,
Elaine O'Rourke
cc: Dr. Rogers

Mrs. Jones has been a principal for four years. She came to Midville when her husband was named the extension agent for Carroll County. She was extremely fortunate to get an administrative position with the schools; and for the most part, she likes her job. Yet the arrival of Dr. Rogers had raised the anxiety levels of all administrators in Midville. Under these conditions. Miss O'Rourke's letter was especially disconcerting. Mrs. Jones realized that she had better do something soon. A telephone call or visit from Dr. Rogers about Miss O'Rourke's letter was inevitable. After thinking about two or three possible courses of action, she decided to meet with Mr. West.

The meeting occurred after school two days following the receipt of Miss

O'Rourke's letter. Mitchell was totally unaware of what was happening. He did not even know about the parental requests that ignited this conflict. Mrs. Jones began the meeting by saying, "Mitchell, we have a bit of a problem."

"What is it?" Mitchell asked.

"Elaine O'Rourke is really steaming because the parents of two of her students requested transfers for their children to your class. Even though they were denied, she thinks that the requests reflect negatively upon her."

Looking puzzled, Mitchell said, "I don't know a thing about this. This is the first I've heard of it."

The principal responded, "Well.I wish I could say it's over—but it's not. She wrote me a letter indicating her belief that the requests are a result of differing standards in the two fifth-grade classrooms. To put it bluntly, she thinks you're too easy on the children. Furthermore, she's demanding that I do something about it. She even sent Dr. Rogers a copy of the letter."

Mrs. Jones expected Mitchell to respond, but he sat there, too stunned to talk. Mrs. Jones broke the silence. "Mitchell, let's try to resolve this quickly. When the superintendent calls, I want to tell him that I already have acted. I want you to start assigning at least one to two hours of homework every evening. I think that should take care of everything. Can I expect your cooperation?" she asked.

THE CHALLENGE: Assume Mitchell's role. How would you respond to Mrs. Jones?

KEY ISSUES FOR STUDY:

1. Identify the options Mitchell has in this situation.
2. Identify environmental factors that you believe affected the behavior of Mrs. Jones and Miss O'Rourke.
3. Analyze Miss O'Rourke's behavior in this case. Would you have behaved in the same way?
4. Do you believe that Mitchell's behavior is congruent with the prevailing philosophy of the school?
5. What positive outcomes can be attained from this situation?
6. If you were Mitchell, would you talk to Miss O'Rourke about this matter? If yes, what would you say? If no, state your reasons for avoiding confrontation.
7. Would you want to be a teacher in Midville? Would you want to work for Mrs. Jones and Dr. Rogers? Please explain your answers.
8. To what extent is Mitchell responsible for this situation?
9. What could Mitchell have done to prevent this incident? What could Mrs. Jones have done to prevent it?
10. If Mitchell conforms without question, how could this affect the students?

SUGGESTED READINGS

Barber, B. (1986). Why students don't need more homework. *Education Digest*, *52*(3), 48–49.

Foyle, H., & Bailey, G. (1986). Homework: Its real purpose. *Clearing House*, *60*, 187–188.

Featherstone, H. (1985). What does homework accomplish? *Principal*, *65*(2), 6–7.

Hill, S., Spencer, S., Alston, R., & Fitzgerald, J. (1986). Homework policies in the schools. *Education*, *107*, 58–70.

O'Donnell, H. (1985). Homework in the elementary school: Eric/RSC. *Reading Teacher*, *39*, 220–222.

Rabbe, P. (1986). Why homework? *Lutheran Education*, *121*, 142–146.

Walberg, H., Paschal, R., & Weinstein, T. (1985). Homework's powerful effects on learning. *Educational Leadership*, *42*(7), 76–79.

CASE 18

Facing the Decisions Imposed by a Teachers' Strike

Karen Washington faces what she believes is the greatest decision of her life. Tomorrow she must decide if she will participate in a teachers' strike. The predicament angers Karen. She sits alone in her newly acquired apartment mulling over her options and trying to determine how she got herself into this situation.

Just four months ago, Karen graduated from North State College after completing her student teaching. Everything seemed magnificent. She had received an outstanding evaluation for student teaching; she was going to graduate summa cum laude; she had four solid job opportunities; and, most important, she was convinced that she had made an excellent career choice. Karen was in love with teaching!

The youngest of four children, Karen had been reared in the industrial area of Pittsburgh. Her father was an ardent union loyalist who, after thirty-one years of employment in the steel mills, was forced to take an early retirement. Her mother, who managed to complete her high school education after she got married, works as a clerk in a meatpacking company—a job she has held for twenty-two years. In the Washington household, education is a high priority. Karen's siblings all attended college. One of her brothers left after his freshman year to join the army, and, after twelve years, has decided to make the military his career. Karen's sister is a nursing supervisor in a suburban hospital and her other brother is finishing his Ph.D. in sociology at the University of Texas.

Karen has a very close relationship with her mother. She would preach to Karen, "Getting your degree is your ticket to job security. Look at what happened to your father. Thirty-one years and they just tell him he has to retire."

As Karen sits in her room pondering the issue before her, memories of home and college are comforting. But she also thinks about the major decision she made just two months ago—accepting a teaching position in Glennville Schools. Karen had applied for four positions. Each school district had pursued her vigorously. In a way, she had been surprised because the districts were located in quite different environments. One of the school systems was large and urban; one was an affluent suburban district; one was a "blue collar" suburb; and Glennville was a quiet, sleepy little community of 5,000 nestled in the mountains of central Pennsylvania. Perhaps it had been her mother's urgings to seek job security that had prompted Karen to select Glennville. After all, it offered the lowest salary of the four.

The first month of teaching had been superb. Karen had a second-grade class with nineteen healthy and happy students. She had become very good friends with the other second-grade teacher, Martha McKewan, a veteran of twenty-seven years in the classroom. To the unending pleasure of her mother, Karen had also become a member of the choir at the local church of Glennville and began dating the assistant pastor, David Simms.

As a matter of routine, Karen had joined the Glennville Teachers' Association (GTA) the first day she reported to work. She hadn't asked any questions—it seemed like the thing to do. About the second week of school, Karen began receiving an association newsletter entitled "Negotiations Update." The publication had made it clear that the GTA was most unhappy with the progress of its salary negotiations with the school board. Discussions in the lunchroom and teacher's lounge centered almost entirely around the contents of the newsletter. It was obvious that tensions were mounting.

During a routine visit with the principal, Mrs. Armand, Karen had raised the issue of negotiations.

"I just don't understand it," Mrs. Armand said. "I've been in this community longer than I care to admit and nothing like this has ever happened before. I really think we're headed for a showdown. The school board has decided to get tough."

Karen had asked, "What do you mean by getting tough?"

Mrs. Armand thought a moment and responded. "We never had negotiations here until five years ago. The board reluctantly participates in the process. Each year they get a little more bitter. This is not a union town. Even though our salaries are not very high, and even though the board knows that, they find it difficult to accept collective bargaining. Maybe they feel they have to teach the GTA a lesson."

Karen was surprised that the situation was so severe. She asked further, "If there is a strike, Mrs. Armand, what do you recommend that I do?"

"Karen, you know I have to be on the board's side in this matter," she responded. "I don't believe in strikes. You have to decide what is best for you. As a first-year teacher, you better be careful."

Two days after her conference with the principal, the officers of the

GTA held a strike vote. Karen did not vote because she was torn by mixed emotions. The teachers voted overwhelmingly to strike. A majority of the teachers believed that the board would not make salary concessions without a strike. The strike would begin in the morning.

Sitting in her room alone now, Karen also recalls other pleas she had made for advice.

Mrs. McKewan, a professional role model for Karen, had told her, "I'm going out on strike. I never thought I would. But this has become a matter of honor and professional integrity."

Karen's recently acquired friend, Reverend Simms, had responded by saying that a strike would not go over very well in the community. "As a first-year teacher, Karen, you could be very vulnerable," he advised.

Karen had reluctantly called home and discussed the matter with her parents. Even they disagreed on what she should do. Her father told her to honor the strike; her mother told her to protect her job.

Ralph Hopson, president of the GTA, had said, "Karen, your best friends are in the GTA. Stand with us and we'll stand behind you. Don't make the mistake of turning your back on your professional colleagues."

All of this would not be so bad if Karen didn't really like her job, the community, and, most important, the children in her classroom. Karen had received two letters from parents urging her not to go on strike. One father had pleaded, "Only the children suffer in a strike. Why should they be made the innocent victims of a political fight?"

Just two weeks ago, everything was so perfect, so rosy. Karen wanted her experiences in Glennville to continue to be positive. Yet she knew she had to make a decision that could change forever her future in this community.

THE CHALLENGE: Place yourself in Karen's position. Will you go out on strike tomorrow morning?

KEY ISSUES FOR STUDY:

1. Identify the positive and negative factors associated with a decision not to become a part of the strike.
2. Identify the positive and negative factors associated with a decision to become a part of the strike.
3. Would you seek advice from any additional sources (i.e., other than those identified in the case) before making your decision: If yes, what sources? Why would you choose these sources?
4. How do personal values affect a decision regarding this matter?
5. Do you think you are placed in an unfair position? Why or why not?
6. If you decide not to go out on strike, what would you tell your peers in the teachers' association?

7. If you decide to go out on strike, what would you communicate (if anything) to the principal?

8. How would you explain your decision to your parents?

9. Are there any options other than striking or not striking? If so, what are they?

10. What, if any, legal issues need to be examined regarding this case?

11. Does the environmental setting, a small town, affect this case? Why or why not?

12. Was it wrong not to vote when the GTA held a strike vote? Explain your answer.

SUGGESTED READINGS

Armstrong, D. G., Henson, K. T., & Savage, T. V. (1989). *Education: An introduction* (3rd ed.) (pp. 283–296). New York: Macmillan.

Jacourt, H., Egan, P., & Slesnick, D. (1987). Can damage suits be brought against strikers and their unions? *Journal of Law & Education, 16*, 203–224.

Kowalski, T. J. (1982). Organizational climate, conflict, and collective bargaining. *Contemporary Education, 54(1)*, 27–30.

Lieberman, M. (1986). *Beyond public education* (pp. 224–227). New York: Praeger.

Long, J. (1986). What to expect during a teacher's strike. *Thrust, 16*, 44–45.

Stinnett, T. M., & Henson, K. T. (1982). *America's public schools in transition* (pp. 263–269; 276–277). New York: Teachers College Press.

CASE 19

Building-level Involvement
in Curriculum Planning

THE SCHOOL DISTRICT

Jefferson County School District is the second largest school system in a rapidly growing southwestern state. There is only one major city in the county, Jeff City, and it is surrounded by myriad suburban developments. The district is recognized for its efforts in desegregation, and also for its successes in developing innovative programs for exceptional children.

Dr. Dominic Bettoli, a midwest transplant, has been superintendent for four years. During this period he has been successful in luring a number of outstanding educators to his central office staff. Among them is Dr. Barbara French, Associate Superintendent for Curriculum. Until last year, Dr. French was a professor at the state university. She has initiated a new program entitled CIDIS (Curriculum Innovation/Development in Schools). The foci of the project are to move curriculum development to the individual school levels and to increase faculty participation in curriculum planning.

Dr. French's effort, based largely upon her writings while in a professorial role, has become the nucleus of Superintendent Bettoli's goals for the next three years. Jefferson County School District is a very heterogeneous school system in terms of the ethnic backgrounds and economic status of its students. The school board has embraced the notion that each school is a unique entity and that, as such, successful programming is best accomplished by planning within the schools themselves. On July 1 of this year, Dr. French's program was formalized in the following school board policy:

Jefferson County School District Policy No. 3.456:
Curriculum Innovation/Development in Schools

Effective immediately, all school sites in the Jefferson County School District are required to develop a master plan for curriculum development and evaluation. Such plans must include provisions assuring participation by teachers, staff, and parents. Written plans must be approved by the school principal, the Associate Superintendent for Curriculum, and the Superintendent of Schools no later than October 31 of each school year. All plans must be in compliance with state mandates and district policies governing instructional programs.

THE SCHOOL

Nicholson Elementary School is located in Jeff City. It is a new facility resulting from the consolidation of Central Elementary (a school that was 80 percent black) and Truman Elementary (a school that was predominantly white—but 30 percent Hispanic). Approximately 25 percent of the students are bused to the school from neighborhoods outside of Jeff City. The school includes four sections per grade level, kindergarten through five.

Dr. Jose Guzman was employed as principal of the school a full year before the building opened. He recently completed his doctorate in education at the state university. In fact, Jose was one of Dr. French's students, and she personally recommended him for this position. Bright and energetic, Dr. Guzman lacks administrative experience and has only three years of teaching experience in an elementary school. At age twenty-nine, he is the youngest principal in the school system. Over the past year he assisted with selecting equipment and the staffing of the school.

Because Nicholson Elementary is the product of consolidation, Dr. Guzman had to give preference to staff from Central Elementary and from Truman Elementary in filling teaching vacancies. This did not concern him unduly because the teachers in the two buildings provided a range of experiences and interests. As it turned out, only two positions at Nicholson were staffed with persons not already employed by the school district. One of these was the assistant principalship. In this slot, Dr. Guzman employed a former classmate from the university, Angela Rodriguez. The other position was a fourth-grade assignment that he filled with a first-year teacher.

Dr. Guzman decided to form a coordinating council to help develop the plan for Nicholson Elementary to meet the requirements of Policy 3.456. He selected six teachers to work with him on the project. To his surprise, three rejected the invitation to participate in this critical assignment. Andrea Brown, a first-grade teacher, responded as follows: "I really would like to help, but my first duty is to my teaching. Changing schools complicates matters. Maybe this idea of curriculum planning at the building level will work. I just don't want to be one of the guinea pigs." Roger Ulchowicz, a fifth-grade teacher, wrote the following note:

Dear Dr. Guzman:

Thank you for the invitation to be a member of the coordinating group for the curriculum development project. I could give you a dozen reasons why I should not participate. You'll discover that I'm a straight shooter. So here it is—I don't do extra work without extra compensation. If you can get me released time or a stipend for this activity, I'll reconsider. Hope you understand.

Roger

Sharon McDaniel, a fourth-grade teacher, gave the following reason for rejecting the invitation: "I really don't know anything about curriculum development. Maybe you should ask someone else."

These unanticipated rejections disappointed Dr. Guzman. He found he had literally to beg teachers to accept the assignment. Eventually all three of the experienced fourth-grade teachers refused to participate. This left him no choice but to approach the first-year teacher.

THE ISSUE

Dr. Guzman called Sylvia Allen, a first-year teacher, into his office on September 10. It was only the second week of school.

He said, "I have a bit of problem here. As you know, Dr. French is the author of a new program called CIDIS. I've decided to put together a coordinating group to develop the required plan for our school. This plan must indicate how we will plan and evaluate curricular offerings and it must be completed in five to six weeks. It also must indicate the ways teachers and parents will be involved in the process. I know it is asking a great deal of you, but I would like you to represent the fourth grade on the coordinating group. You may already know that all the other fourth-grade teachers said they wouldn't do it. Normally I wouldn't ask a first-year teacher to do this."

Sylvia is by her nature a shy person. She didn't welcome the tension provided by this situation. Cautiously she asked about the expectations of this assignment and explained that she knew very little about curriculum planning.

Dr. Guzman explained, "The task of the coordinating group is to determine a structure for the planning process. That is, the coordinating group simply lays out a structure permitting a much larger group to engage in planning." He told Sylvia that her job would be to suggest answers to the following questions.

a. What will be the role of teachers? Of parents?
b. When will this work be done?
c. What types of incentives can be given to teachers and parents to induce them to participate?

THE CHALLENGE: You are the first-year teacher. Think about the task and prepare an answer for Dr. Guzman.

KEY ISSUES FOR STUDY:

1. What are the benefits of accepting Dr. Guzman's invitation to be a member of the coordinating group?
2. What are the potential problems associated with accepting Dr. Guzman's invitation?
3. Do you think the principal should rethink his idea of a coordinating group in light of the fact that so many teachers have turned him down? Explain your answer.
4. Assess the merits of the entire concept of CIDIS.
5. What actions could have been taken by the administration to better facilitate implementation of Policy 3.456?
6. Are there any advantages to including a first-year teacher in this coordinating group? Explain your answer.
7. What do you think the refusal of so many teachers to be part of the coordinating group means for the implementation of Policy 3.456?
8. Discuss the ramifications of an alternate approach by the principal, in which he would have *required* specified teachers to be members of the coordinating group.
9. Assume that Dr. Guzman mandates your participation. Develop answers to his questions relative to participation, logistics, and incentives.

SUGGESTED READINGS

Arends, R. I. (1983). Beginning teachers as learners. *Journal of Educational Research*, *76*, 235–242.

Bailey, G. (1986). Curriculum development—A method to define roles, procedures. *NASSP Bulletin*, *70*, 50–55.

Earle, R. (1985). Teachers as instructional developers. *Education Technology*, *25*, 15–18.

Fagan, M. M., & Walter, G. (1983). Mentoring among teachers. *Education Digest*, *49*, 51–53.

Hawthorne, R. (1986). The professional teacher's dilemma: Balancing autonomy and obligation. *Educational Leadership*, *44*, 34–35.

Neely, A. (1985). Teacher planning: Where has it been? Where is it now? *Action in Teacher Education*, *7*, 25–29.

Perry, P. (1986). A building-based project approach to instructional improvement. *Clearing House*, *59*, 363–365.

Samples, B. (1984). Reflections on curriculum, teachers, and teaching. *Educational Leadership*, *41*, 64–67.

Schultz, E. (1983). The nuts and bolts of curriculum development. *Thrust*, *13*, 43–44.

CASE 20

Trying on Teaching Styles

The Westside Alternative School in Lake City is an oasis for students identified as potential dropouts or "push outs." It is a place where students can vote on important issues during the weekly "Town Meeting." Students design many of their learning activities, and they can pursue independent study on almost any topic. While students' performance is evaluated, it is done through oral and written feedback—no letter grades are given. Everyone is on a first-name basis, even the principal, Nate Evans. Dress is relaxed. Most teachers and students wear jeans, T-shirts, sweatshirts, and casual footwear.

Nate started the school seventeen years ago. He had been given this opportunity after a group of parents had petitioned the school board to offer an alternative program for students "turned off" by the traditional school experience. Given the success of this small, public school of three hundred secondary students—the school was mandated by the board of education to remain at or below that number—Nate and his staff had become empowered to select teachers to replace anyone who left. An interview team was organized, composed of students, teachers, and parents. New teachers could be hired by majority vote. The hiring process was viewed as essential to maintaining a staff with similar interests and philosophies.

Kurt Kendrick had been somewhat intimidated by the interview process. He had been surprised by the thoroughness of the questions. Even more surprising was the fact that students and parents were involved. Having to teach a class while the interview team observed had tested his nerves. Yet he was ecstatic when he learned he had been hired. He felt he had been welcomed into a new family. There was a feeling of warmth, enthusiasm, and joy he had not sensed in other interviews he had had. He looked forward to teaching art at Westside.

"What we like most about you," Nate Evans told him, "is the fact you appear comfortable with teaching—relaxed, open, and caring."

Kurt felt lucky to land a job at Westside. There were five other alternative schools in Lake City, but none had the history or reputation of Westside. Located in a low socioeconomic neighborhood near the industrial hub of this large, urban city in the southwest, the school was housed in an abandoned warehouse constructed in the early 1920s. The building was filled with discarded furniture—overstuffed chairs, couches, tables, and assorted pieces of furniture of every shape and size. This array of accumulated mismatched furniture resulted largely because students were permitted to bring their own desks and chairs to the school. Walls were filled with graffiti. These "extended chalkboards" reflected the changing moods of the school's inhabitants.

There is no newspaper or yearbook at Westside. "There's no reason for one," Nate claimed. "Students have free expression here, so they don't need another outlet."

Westside appealed to Kurt for several reasons. He was a maverick himself. He had studied violin for fifteen years, and everyone in his family had expected him to become a professional musician. After his second concert, in the year before his freshman year at Central University, he had decided he did not want to do what others expected him to do. Between his junior and senior year at Central he took a year off and worked his way through South America—moving from place to place as earnings permitted. This move had shocked his family as much as the earlier one. Upon Kurt's graduation, his father, a wealthy businessman in the East, had "reserved" a teaching and coaching position at a private academy in his home town. Again, Kurt disappointed his family by not only moving 2,700 miles away but also by accepting a teaching position in a school his father considered a "dilapidated jailhouse for juvenile delinquents."

Early during his first semester at Westside, Kurt discovered he was not as prepared for the free and unstructured environment as he thought. He had planned carefully for his art classes. Before school began he had borrowed a truck from a friend and collected scrap lumber, discarded metal, rubber tires, railroad ties, cardboard boxes, and plastic, and had purchased paints and oils he found on sale. A massive storage area in the school building had been converted into an art area. Large tubs, hot and cold water, and extensive cabinet space made the area nearly ideal.

He organized each class period around a specific timetable. For the first five minutes he reviewed what had been accomplished the preceding day. For the next five to ten minutes he lectured or "previewed" theories or principles underlying an art activity the students were expected to accomplish. On the first day of the week and on the last day of the week he tried to find a film, filmstrip, or other visual media to illustrate the kind of product he wanted to inspire the students to create. Each day toward the end of the period, before students put away their work, he organized a brief discussion around a couple of students' efforts. Such "evaluation sessions," as he thought of them, were intended to build high expectations, cooperation, and creative thinking. While he used a variety of instructional methods, including demonstrations of his own work (he never asked students to do anything he would not do also), the routine was fixed.

He sailed smoothly through the first two weeks. It was during the third week that what seemed to be a well-oiled machine began to sputter. It started when Alicia Raines approached him after his Monday class.

"Mr. Kendrick, may I talk to you?" she asked.

"Sure, but we'll need to hurry. I have another class coming in," he responded. "What is it?"

"Well, I don't know how to say this," she hesitated. "I like your class. You're a good teacher. And the other students in your classes like you too. But several of us are afraid things aren't going to work out."

"Why?" Kurt said with a look of surprise.

"Your classes are becoming monotonous," she said.

"I admit I'm organized, but I try to vary what we do," he responded. "And I allow students to choose the kinds of art projects they do."

"Maybe you're too organized. Give us some slack," she remarked.

The students in his next period class began to enter.

"Alicia, why don't you get some of the other students together after school today so we can talk about this. Is that possible?" Kurt said with concern.

"Sure," Alicia said. "Here in your room? 3:30?"

"Yes, that will be fine. See you later," Kurt responded.

After school, a dozen students came to Mr. Kendrick's room. Three of them were sophomores, two were juniors, and the rest were seniors. For forty-five minutes they discussed their concerns about his teaching. Most of the students' comments focused on two points. One was that Mr. Kendrick seemed more rigid as a teacher than he had during the interview process. The second focused on the students' preferred approaches to being taught.

Some of the students said they need to be left alone for longer periods of time to work on their projects. A few of the students indicated they wanted to work in pairs or teams. Other students suggested that he provide a variety of ways for students to learn in class. As one student said: "We want to choose what we study. That's why we came to Westside. Let us decide. All the other teachers do."

THE CHALLENGE: What should Mr. Kendrick do?

THE ISSUES FOR STUDY:

1. How serious a problem do you believe Mr. Kendrick has? Explain your answer.
2. Do you believe he should have met with the students? Why or why not?
3. Does Mr. Kendrick have a responsibility to alter his instructional approaches based on students' concerns?

4. What are possible positive outcomes from altering his instructional approaches?

5. What are possible negative outcomes?

6. Should Mr. Kendrick seek advice from someone else in the school? If so, who? And what kinds of advice should he seek? If not, why not?

SUGGESTED READINGS

Dawe, H. (1984). Teaching: A performing art. *Phi Delta Kappan*, *68*(8), 548–552.

Guskey, T., & Gates, S. (1986). Synthesis of research on the effects of mastery learning in elementary and secondary classrooms. *Educational Leadership*, *43*(8), 73–80.

Hyman, R., & Rosoff, B. (1984). Matching learning and teaching styles. *Theory into Practice*, *23*, 35–43.

Kane, P. (1987). Public or independent schools: Does where you teach make a difference? *Phi Delta Kappan*, *69*(4), 286–289.

Karweit, N. (1984). Time-on-task reconsidered: Synthesis of research on time and learning. *Educational Leadership*, *41*(8), 32–35.

McFaul, S. (1983). An examination of direct instruction. *Educational Leadership*, *40*(7), 67–69.

Meier, D. (1987). Central Park East: An alternative story. *Phi Delta Kappan*, *68*(10), 753–757.

Nathan, J. (1987). Results and future prospects of state efforts to increase choice among schools. *Phi Delta Kappan*, *68*(10), 746–752.

Raywid, M. (1984). Synthesis of research on schools of choice. *Educational Leadership*, *41*(7), 71–78.

Rosenshine, B. (1986). Synthesis of research on explicit teaching. *Educational Leadership*, *43*(7), 60–69.

CASE 21

The Teacher and Child Abuse

There were some days when Tim Lawson just didn't think 3:15 P.M. would ever arrive. Today was different. He sat staring at the wall clock while his fifth-grade students completed their math assignments. At 3:45 Tim had a meeting with Elaine Sylvia, the school system's social worker; and if he could wave his magic wand, the clock would never reach the dismissal time of 3:15.

Since graduating from Cromwell College seven months ago, Tim has adjusted rather well to the responsibilities of being a teacher. His parents are educators, and he never had much doubt about his career choice. Being a good student and campus leader helped Tim get a position in one of the more affluent and prestigious school districts in this northwestern state.

Apple Valley School District, located in a suburban setting near the state capital, has a high school, middle school, and four elementary schools. The district has the highest salary schedule in the state. Most of the residents are college graduates and the average price of a home in the community is $175,000.

Tim enjoys his students. The vast majority are motivated. They come to school well fed and neatly dressed. Discipline is not a particular problem, and overall the students do quite well on standardized ability and achievement tests. Tim appreciates the fact that he can devote most of his energy to instructional preparation and teaching. Unlike teachers working in districts with complex social and economic problems, he isn't forced to spend countless hours on matters unrelated to instruction. In fact, this is the main reason he accepted a position in Apple Valley.

There is, however, one student, David, who presents a special challenge to Tim. Although he is a capable student, David rarely reaches his potential.

He is somewhat withdrawn and perceived by peers as a loner. In a number of ways he seems different from the other children. Yet compared to his classmates, there is nothing different about his physical appearance. He wears expensive clothes and comes to school neatly groomed.

David's continuing achievement problems prompted Tim to request a conference with David's parents. Over the last three months, two such conferences were held. Each time David's mother appeared alone dressed in jeans and wearing, in Tim's opinion, an excessive amount of makeup. Her behavior was aggressive. She defended her son relentlessly regardless of the issue. Although David doesn't stand out physically among his peers, the mother certainly looks and acts differently from the other mothers Tim has met since coming to Apply Valley. The first conference did not accomplish much. Nevertheless, Tim was able to make several suggestions regarding greater parental involvement in David's schoolwork.

During the second conference, Tim expressed his disappointment that David was not exhibiting progress either in his studies or in establishing friendships among his classmates.

"Look," the mother responded, "let's cut the idle talk and get to the point. I had hoped that since you were new to this community you might treat David fairly. I was hoping you might be different—that you wouldn't be influenced by his father's reputation. But I can see that the gossip has already affected you."

Tim had no idea what she was talking about and was uncertain if he should ask for clarification. He finally asked, "What do you mean? I know virtually nothing about your husband—or you, for that matter. David's records simply indicate that his father is in private business."

With a disbelieving smile, the mother answered, "I suppose you don't read the papers. You don't know that his father owns taverns, adult bookstores, and X-rated theaters?" Tim really had not known this, but he quickly assessed how this fact could affect the residents of Apple Valley (and ultimately, peer behavior toward David in his classroom).

Ever since that conference, Tim has exerted an inordinate amount of his time and energy to create social and educational opportunities for David. He believes the boy needs to find success—any kind of success. Three days ago David arrived at school with the left side of his face covered with bruises. During recess, Tim asked David to remain in class, and he questioned the boy about his injuries. David would only say that he had fallen. Being quite concerned, Tim took him to see Mrs. Barnes, the school nurse. She discovered that Tim also had bruises on his chest and legs. Mrs. Barnes didn't believe David's explanation regarding the injuries. She insisted that the case be turned over to the school district social worker.

That day, after school, Tim had a meeting with Miss Sylvia, the social worker; Mrs. Hines, the principal; and Mrs. Barnes. It was agreed that Miss Sylvia would pursue the matter and interview the boy the next morning.

Following the interview, Tim was asked to meet with Miss Sylvia. The social worker started the conversation by exchanging routine information about her role in such matters. She asked Tim several basic questions about David's work in the classroom, his relationship with peers, and inquired if the boy had any special interests.

Then Miss Sylvia got right to the point. "I think this boy has been abused by his parents, more specifically by his father. During our session, David admitted that his father has a bad temper and sometimes hits him and his younger sister. Occasionally, he even slaps his wife. This guy is in the news all the time. He is a big-time racketeer. You know that, don't you?"

Tim responded, "I didn't know about him until the last conference with his wife. She told me what he does for a living."

Miss Sylvia continued, "I plan to go after this bully. It won't be easy. He's got more lawyers than you and I have pencils. Before I can pursue this matter further, I need something from you suggesting your concern about the parents."

"What do you mean?" asked Tim.

"Something that says they're not the best citizens in town. You met with the mother several times. Did she look like a good mother? You said she showed up in jeans. I met her once at a conference when David was in second grade. She looked like a chorus girl—not a mother. Can you imagine what David's home life must be like?"

Tim was puzzled and asked again, "What do you want me to do?"

"Write a letter saying that you suspect that this child was abused by his parents. That gives me added leverage to pursue this matter. If I can force this thing, I bet that I'm right. The father physically abused this kid."

Tim sat silent for a moment. He collected his thoughts. Frustrated by his uncertainty, he said, "Let me sleep on it. I'll meet with you after school tomorrow and give you my answer. Is 3:45 all right with you?"

Looking disappointed, Miss Sylvia said decisively, "You know you have responsibilities as a teacher. If you don't look out for these kids, who will? Yes, I'll see you tomorrow at 3:45."

Tim, lost in thoughts concerning the previous day, looked up and realized that the clock was just a few ticks away from 3:15. He had to meet with the social worker in thirty minutes. How could this have happened in Apple Valley?

THE CHALLENGE: Put yourself in Tim's place. What would you tell Miss Sylvia?

KEY ISSUES FOR STUDY:

1. Identify any resources you could use to arrive at a decision in this case.
2. In your deliberations regarding the social worker's request, what would have been the advantages and disadvantages of trying to talk to

    a. David?
    b. the principal?
    c. the parents?
    d. the superintendent?
    e. other teachers?
    f. a lawyer?
    g. a minister?
    h. a representative from a social agency?

3. Do you think Miss Sylvia is making a reasonable request of Tim? Why or why not?

4. Do you perceive any inconsistencies in the request made by Miss Sylvia? Is she asking for judgments or facts? Explain your answer.

5. Are there potential dangers in meeting Miss Sylvia's request? If yes, what are they?

6. Draft a letter responding to Miss Sylvia. Be sure that your letter offers a justification for your ultimate decision either to write a letter suggesting possible child abuse or to refuse to write such a letter.

7. What, if any, recommendations could you make to Miss Sylvia about pursuing the case without a letter from you?

8. Discuss legal and professional issues relevant to this case.

9. Was Tim being realistic in believing that places like Apple Valley are free from problems that plague less economically advantaged communities? Explain your answer.

10. This case deals with physical abuse. Identify other forms of child abuse that may occur.

SUGGESTED READINGS

Beezer, B. (1985). Reporting child abuse and neglect: Your responsibility and your protections. *Phi Delta Kappan, 66*, 434–436.

Boucher, C., & Weinstein, S. (1985). Training professionals to be powerful and collaborative. *Contemporary Education, 56*, 130–136.

Child abuse: Some words of caution. (1987). *American Teacher, 72*, 24.

Fontana, V. (1987). Child abuse—one sign of a troubled society. *Momentum, 18*, 24–26.

Hurwitz, B. (1985). How to counsel children. *Instructor, 94*, 77–78.

Lynn, S. (1985). Suspicion: Child abuse. *Instructor, 94*, 76–77.

Meddin, B., & Rosen, A. (1986). Child abuse and neglect: Prevention and reporting. *Young Children, 41*, 26–30.

Racusin, R., & Felsman, J. (1986). Reporting child abuse: The ethical obligation to inform parents. *Journal of the American Academy of Child Psychiatry, 25*(4), 485–489.

Tanner, C. (1985). Helping abused children: Can we? How? *Education, 105*, 354–399.

Turbett, J., & O'Toole, R. (1983). Teachers' recognition and reporting of child abuse. *Journal of School Health, 53*, 605–609.

Zirkel, P., & Gluckman, I. (1986). Reporting child abuse. *Principal, 65*, 47–48.

CASE 22

Coping with a Negative Faculty

THE SCHOOL DISTRICT

Lincoln County School District is among the twenty largest school systems in the country. During the period of rapid school population growth in the early 1970s, Lincoln County had almost two hundred schools. Its southern coastal location has made Lincoln County School District unique in two important ways. First, when rapid school enrollments peaked for the rest of the country, redistricting and busing laws caused Lincoln's enrollment to increase. A second unique aspect of the Lincoln County area is its reputation as a retirement heaven. The warm climate, clear blue skies, and the white sandy beaches attract a constant flow of middle-aged and senior citizens from throughout the northern states. Because these residents have no school-age children, most of them are reluctant to vote for any referendum that would give support to the schools. Most harbor the "We've done our share" attitude. Truthfully, because most of these older residents are on a "fixed income" many of them really cannot afford the tax increases needed to operate a quality school district.

THE SCHOOL

Coastal Shores High School is located in an affluent suburban community, one of the wealthiest in the country. Here, property in both business and residential zones is appraised by linear footage. A single vacant residential lot often sells for hundreds of thousands of dollars. Throughout the 1950s and

1960s this plush community was the home of some of the wealthiest people in the country. Many older residents moved to the area when the land sold at a small fraction of its current value; others moved there from other sections of the country. Strict building codes and high prices shielded the residents from the rest of the world.

During the 1950s and 1960s, the student body at Coastal Shores High was made up mostly of children of local families who could afford to live in the area and of wealthy northerners who, insisting on having the very best schools available for their children, boarded their children to enable them to attend this outstanding school. Coastal Shores High had a national reputation as one of the very best high schools in the country. The administrators and teachers proudly announced that their students won more academic scholarships and national awards than any other students. After each standardized test was administered, the newspaper ran a full center page with a chart listing all the standardized achievement test scores of each of the more than two hundred high schools in the state. The chart contained the national mean achievement scores, enabling comparisons among the local schools and between them and the nation as a whole.

But the school busing laws of the 1960s and 1970s finally penetrated the walls that shielded Coastal Shores from the rest of the population. Suddenly, the student body experienced a rapid shift from the very wealthy Anglos to include a balanced mix of students representing more than fifty cultures, the majority from low-income families. Predominant minority groups included black Americans, Cubans, Bahamians, Haitians, and Jamaicans. Coastal Shores' faculty and student body experienced total fragmentation. The faculty's sense of pride was replaced by indignant feelings of, "How could this happen to us? Why did they do this to our school?"

THE INCIDENT

Amy Worley was excited to receive a teaching position in a school that had distinguished itself nationally. A social studies major, Amy welcomed the opportunity to work with students from so many cultural backgrounds. Her assignment included two sections of tenth-grade social studies and three sections of eleventh-grade American history. Like most first-year teachers, Amy had developed many lesson plans that she wanted to "try out." In her American history class she was especially eager to experiment with some simulations and games that she had personally developed in her methods classes.

Right away, Amy noticed among her students a sense of complacency; she also observed several behavioral patterns that she had not expected. Many of the students seemed to be isolating themselves in their own individual worlds. Most of the complacent students usually sat near the back of the room. When called on to participate, they seldom had any idea of what was happening in the class, and their knowledge of the content was dismally poor. Also, several students in each of her classes seemed particularly rude to their classmates. For example, each time a girl sharpened her pencil, the boys would often whistle and make exaggerated nonverbal gestures to draw attention to the girls' hip movements. The behavior of some of the girls was no better.

But Amy felt that she could handle these distractions. She knew that many of the students just wanted more attention, and she had many excellent student activities planned into her future lessons. In all, she felt optimistic; and having recently made the transition from student teacher to real teacher, Amy was thankful for the opportunity to have her own classes.

Each school day was so busy—even hectic—that Amy looked forward to her planning period. This was a time to reflect on her classes and a time to share her new experiences with her fellow teachers. For the first few weeks she did just that; each planning period was spent in the teacher's lounge. After a few weeks had passed, Amy noticed something that she had not been aware of in the past. Each day she had been so excited that she had spent each planning period talking about her classes, her students, and some of the simulation games she had recently discovered. Amy's enthusiasm for her assignment and her confidence in her own ability to turn these students around and make them more studious were reflected in her comments. As she discussed the games that she had selected, she displayed so much enthusiasm that her colleagues expected her to begin at any moment teaching the games to them.

Having learned in her methods classes that simulations and games are effective strategies for motivating student interest, Amy was planning to introduce a game called *Conflict*, which focuses on a crisis that erupts in 1999. This game instructs students that the nations of the world have developed three international councils with an international policy for peace. Amy hoped that the game would increase the level of motivation of her apathetic students while making them sensitive to the need to work together cooperatively.

Another game Amy had prepared to use in her social studies classes is called *Politica*, which presents a major international crisis set in Latin America and involves major international conflicts. If for some reason her students failed to relate to these games, Amy had identified a back-up strategy, a game titled *Yes, But Not Here*. This game presents an urban conflict over where a condominium for the elderly should be located. And Amy had chosen a special game for her American history class. *Simulation of American Government* places students in roles found in various branches of the U.S. government. Amy wondered whether she should even mention to her fellow teachers her plans to use those games. She feared it might cause resentment toward her for her level of enthusiasm. For the first time, Amy realized that she had not been giving her colleagues an opportunity to discuss their own classes.

When she finally slowed down enough to listen, Amy discovered that her fellow teachers were saying things about their students and about the school that she did not want to hear. Mr. King, an English teacher, and Mrs. Holland, a psychology/physical education teacher, were rapidly approaching retirement. Their conversations vacillated between discussions about the good old days when the students respected their elders, and particularly their teachers, and a more recent concern over the pending legislation that would encourage early retirement. Mr. Arnold and Mrs. Huff, both physical education/health teachers, were critical of some of the other teachers who had begun an experimental drug-abuse prevention program. A common attitude among these four teachers was what they perceived as a current state of hopelessness, a condition that they blamed on modern society, the current laws, and a generation of apathetic students and parents. In all of their comments, Amy heard a clear message of pessimism. Some of the teachers were still openly bitter and resentful over the changes that they had seen occur in the school without their having had opportunities to provide any input. Each day, Amy talked less and listened more. Soon her fellow teachers began to ask her to agree with their views. Amy wanted to be friends with the other teachers, but she abhorred their negativism. She wondered what she should do.

THE CHALLENGE: Amy must make some decisions. Her choices could affect her future in the Lincoln County School District. Put yourself in her place as you consider the following issues.

KEY ISSUES FOR STUDY:

1. To what extent must a teacher let the climate of the school affect the climate in the teacher's own classes?
2. How much rudeness should a teacher permit students to display toward their classmates?
3. Do teachers really need to share "social" time with their fellow teachers?
4. Like Amy, many beginning teachers are very enthusiastic. What problems can this cause?
5. What possible results can occur when a teacher hears negative comments each day from other teachers?
6. What are the possible dangers of joining in on the negativism of other teachers and becoming a complainer, if a teacher doesn't really feel that way?
7. What additional information is needed before deciding on a course of action?
8. How should this knowledge affect Amy's behavior?

SUGGESTED READINGS

Bleecher, H. (1985). Why teachers carry out orders. *Education, 105,* 333–336.
Hassenpflug, A. (1986). Teacher-administrator cooperation—A necessity for the effective school. *NASSP Bulletin, 70,* 38–41.

Henson, Kenneth T. (1987). *Methods and strategies for teaching in secondary and middle schools*. (See Appendix D: Directory of simulation materials; also see Chapter 5, Simulation games.) White Plains, NY: Longman.

Johnston, G. S., & Venable, B. P. (1986). A study of teacher loyalty to the principal: Rule administration and hierarchical influences of the principal. *Educational Administration Quarterly*, *22*, 4–27.

Nygren, M. (1987). Professional ethics in the field of education. *Illinois Teacher of Home Economics*, *30*, 139–142.

Rich, J. M. (1985). The role of professional ethics in teacher education. *Action in Teacher Education*, *7*, 21–24.

CASE 23

The Father with AIDS

Teaching at Carver Middle School is a real challenge. The principal, Malcolm Bivens, once said, "Every teacher in America ought to spend nine months working at Carver so that they can learn professional humility."

The school is located one-half mile from the business district of a large midwestern city. Noise and air pollution further diminish the aesthetic quality of the educational setting within the three-story brick structure that is almost fifty years old. A high fence encircling the drab brick rectangle seems to be more appropriate for a penal institution than for an environment where children are to be motivated to learn. Every ethnic slur imaginable can be found in bright colors on the sidewalk—most written with misspelled words.

Denise Jackson chose freely and willingly to become a part of this un-inviting environment. Maybe she could have found a job teaching learning-disabled children in a better neighborhood or a better community but she never really tried. Besides teaching, Denise has a burning desire to coach gymnastics. When Professor Don Baker, her supervisor for student teaching at the university, told her about the job at Carver, she never hesitated to apply. Even though she was familiar with the school's dreadful reputation, she realized that is was one place where she could do the two things she loved— teach and coach.

Carver Middle School is a melting pot. At one time the students in the school were primarily children of European immigrants, but in recent years the enrollment has become extremely heterogeneous in terms of ethnic and racial composition.

Denise has a class of fourteen children diagnosed as learning disabled. Her students came from low-income families. They range in age from twelve to fourteen. The students spend about 75 percent of their school day in this self-contained program (they are mainstreamed into physical education, home economics/industrial education, art, and music). A half-time instructional aide is assigned to Denise.

The first three months of the school year were difficult, but not unlike what Denise had anticipated. She found her students a constant challenge to her teaching abilities. In mid-November she started her coaching assignment in gymnastics. As Christmas approached, Denise felt that she would, indeed, come through her first year with sound mind and body.

On Thursday, December 10, at exactly 10:48 A.M., Denise was summoned to the principal's office via the intercom in her room. For some strange reason, she felt extremely uncomfortable. She had met with Principal Bivens on numerous occasions, and his fatherly approach made her feel welcome and safe in these discomforting environs. Yet she sensed that this meeting was going to be different. Her instinctive feelings proved correct.

As Denise entered the office, Malcolm Bivens was wearing his usual smile. Nothing seemed to faze Mr. Bivens. "He's probably seen it all," thought Denise to herself.

"Miss Jackson, how are you today?" he asked, rising to greet her.

"Everything seems to be going well and I'm even finding time to start my Christmas shopping; but somehow I don't think you called me here to talk about that," she answered.

Suddenly the smile on Mr. Bivens's face dissolved. "You're right. I'm afraid it's something that is potentially serious," he said, "I just got a call from Dr. Martinez at the Board of Health. The father of one of your students has been diagnosed as having AIDS."

"Which student?" Denise asked immediately.

"Sandra Bell. Poor Sandra, she's been through so much and now this," Mr. Bivens sighed.

Denise sat down. She wasn't sure if she should start asking questions, act calm and collected, or panic. Unable to decide, she just kept fidgeting, waiting for Mr. Bivens to resume the conversation.

"Dr. Martinez is a personal friend. I'm not sure he was supposed to tell me what I just shared with you. In any event, I think we have to keep this thing quiet. If the word gets out, parents of other students are apt to panic. I don't even want other teachers to hear about this. Sandra is in Mr. Hopnill's art class, Mrs. Parento's music class, and Mrs. McNally's physical education class. Maybe in time I'll tell them about this. But for now, I want you to keep this information to yourself."

"Mr. Bivens, I feel very uncomfortable about this. Besides keeping quiet, are there other things you want me to do?" she inquired.

"I'm going to ask Dr. Martinez to get some materials about AIDS for you to read. Being informed is something all of our teachers need to do. Legally, I don't think there is anything we can do. So, we'll conduct business as usual here at Carver. Of course, we'll keep our eyes open," he concluded.

Denise slowly rose and walked out of the principal's office—dejected, concerned, and feeling sorry for Sandra and herself.

THE CHALLENGE: Determine what Denise should do about this situation.

KEY ISSUES FOR STUDY:

1. Develop a list of options for Denise.
2. What problems could Denise encounter if she does exactly what the principal instructed her to do?
3. Suppose that Denise decides to contact the student's other three teachers (art, music, and physical education) and shares with them the conversation she had with the principal. What are the advantages and disadvantages of this course of action?
4. Identify resources that could be of assistance to Denise in this matter.
5. Do any factors related to this case make you feel uncomfortable?
6. Supposes that Denise calls the school superintendent and asks for advice. What are the advantages and disadvantages of this approach?
7. Identify any potential legal issues related to this case.
8. Should Denise tell her aide about this situation: Why or why not?
9. In what ways does the environmental setting of this case influence your behavior?

SUGGESTED READINGS

Beckham, J. (1986). The AIDS dilemma: Recent court decisions place a burden of persuasion on the public schools. *NASSP Bulletin, 70*, 91–95.

Black, J. (1986). AIDS: Preschool and school issues. *Journal of School Health, 56*, 93–95.

Brick, P. (1987). AIDS: Educating for survival. *Educational Leadership, 44*(7), 78–79.

Keough, K. E., & Seaton, G. (1988). Superintendents' views on AIDS: A national survey. *Phi Delta Kappan, 69*(5), 358–361.

Maifair, L. (1987). How to handle those sensitive questions. *Learning, 15*(7), 56–57.

Moberly, W. (1987). When AIDS hits home. *Principal, 67*, 46.

Price, J. (1985). High school students' perceptions and misperceptions of AIDS. *Journal of School Health, 55*, 107–109.

Price, J. (1986). AIDS, the schools, and policy issues. *Journal of School Health, 56*, 137–140.

Recommended guidelines for dealing with AIDS in the schools from the National Education Association. (1986). *Journal of School Health, 56*, 129–130.

Strike, K., & Soltis, J. (1986). Who broke the fish tank? and other ethical dilemmas. *Instructor, 95*(6), 36–39.

A Teacher Is Dedicated to Promoting Creativity

THE COMMUNITY

Hudson Heights is an urban residential and business area within the metropolitan New York City area. On a clear day from some locations in Hudson Heights residents can see the Statue of Liberty. To visitors, it is clear that most residents of the community are not enjoying the wealth that they see every day. Row after row of run-down government housing with little or no lawn space forces children to play in the streets. Attempts to reestablish a park have proven financially impossible. Most streets are littered with fast-food wrappers, bottles, and cans. In the business district, there seems to be a liquor store on almost every corner. Signs remind vandals that they are under constant crime-watch surveillance, but many of the signs have been defaced with spray paint. One drive through the community tells the visitor that this is what Plato predicted over two thousand years ago when, in his book *The Republic*, he alerted readers about the decay that would occur when urban communities became too congested.

THE SCHOOL

Hudson Elementary appears as old as the city itself. The aged building has suffered fifty very long years of vandalism. It stands like an old general—scarred from its attacks, yet stubbornly refusing defeat. The inscription above the front door reads IN SEARCH OF TRVTH. Mr. Marshall, the new principal, is a strong disciplinarian who equates good teaching with learning those facts that will lead to a good job. He used the first faculty meeting to advise the teachers that he will be visiting all classes and to remind them that he believes in traditional teaching methods.

The hallways at Hudson Elementary are dark and narrow; like the classrooms, they have high ceilings. The old varnish and wood stain on the walls and floors have blackened over the years. All things considered, the general physical appearance of the building can accurately be described as depressing.

But the preceding observation describes how Hudson Elementary School appears to an outsider. Sandy Mears, a fifth-grade teacher at Hudson, has an entirely different perception of the school. To Sandy, Hudson Elementary is a beautiful place. She would agree that the varnish on the walls and floor is dark and unattractive, like the rest of the building, but to Sandy the physical appearance of the school is only a minor, insignificant part. To understand Sandy's perspective, one would need to visit one of her classes.

Once inside Sandy's classroom it is obvious why for her the unattractive appearance of the building fades in importance. Her room promotes enthusiasm. In it busy students are having fun while they study science. Although most of them come from low socioeconomic backgrounds, these students feel good about themselves. They know that they are capable, not because they have unusually high innate abilities—for they are average students—but the difference is that Sandy knows how to help students discover their potentialities.

THE INCIDENT

In her teacher education program, Sandy became interested in creativity as a field of study. This began when a visiting professor conducted a workshop for her language arts methods course. As a participant in the workshop, Sandy learned about several student activities that teachers can use to help students develop their creative abilities. As required projects for her other methods courses, Sandy chose to develop similar activities to enable her future students to become more creative.

Sandy's sixth-grade science class is a good example. The current unit of study focuses on rivers, a topic that the group is also currently studying in their social studies class. At the front of the room is a table surrounded by several students. On the table is a box of large drinking straws, a few pounds of modeling clay, a set of scales, and a stack of books. Several pairs of students are working independently of the other students. Each two-person team is designing a bridge. The object of their challenge is to see which team can design the strongest bridge, using only six ounces of clay and twelve straws. A few teams have already completed their bridge and are now testing it to see how many books it will support.

Another table holds several trays of water, some modeling clay, and a jar of marbles. These students are also working in pairs. Their challenge is to use only three ounces of modeling clay to build a boat that has greater buoyancy than those built by their classmates. When the pairs of students complete designing and constructing their boat, they will test it to see whether it floats and, if so, how many marbles the boat will support before sinking.

Throughout the room, groups of students are conducting similar activities. At each table, students are carefully recording the results of all teams. At the end of the hour students will rotate to a different table until all students have participated in all of the projects. The winners of each project will explain why they designed their project as they did. Sandy will ask specific questions to get students to think further about the tasks. Some of her favorite questions are: What were the results? Why did this occur? How could you improve your project? If you could have one additional material to use in designing or constructing the project, what material would you choose? Why? Sandy also insists that it is essential for the students to ask questions. She believes that learning how to ask the right question is as important as knowing how to find the right answer.

Sandy tries never to miss a chance to recognize her students' accomplishments, but she never gives false praise. She recognizes student success orally and visually. All winning projects are displayed for others to see. Her goal is to have something belonging to every student on display all the time. Sandy groups students so that all will have an equal chance to develop a winning project. She proudly points out that some of her students whose test scores are consistently low succeed in building winning projects. After Mr. Marshall's visit to her class, Sandy's concern over his comments during the recent faculty meeting is understandable. During the meeting, Mr. Marshall clearly communicated that he would not tolerate unorthodox teaching methods, for according to Mr. Marshall, "Recent studies have shown that direct instruction and time on task are producing the most achievement in classrooms across the country." Sandy has begun worrying about Mr. Marshall's forthcoming visit to her classroom. She wonders how she can best plan for the anticipated conflict that may arise.

THE CHALLENGE: Put yourself in Sandy's place as you consider the following issues and questions.

KEY ISSUES FOR STUDY:

1. How can teachers group students to stimulate creativity?
2. For each of your disciplines, describe an activity that would stimulate creativity.
3. Choose one creative activity (which may or may not be one that Sandy used) and make a list of questions to promote further thinking.
4. How can teachers motivate students to share the teacher's enthusiasm?

5. List some ways that teachers can show their enthusiasm for their subject.
6. Why is it important that students ask questions?
7. List some school characteristics other than physical appearance that shape students' and teachers' impressions of their school.
8. How can Sandy convince her principal that promoting creativity is a worthy goal?
9. How important is each of the following:
   a. The physical appearance of this school is depressing.
   b. These students come from low socioeconomic homes.
   c. Sandy uses an interdisciplinary approach.
   d. Sandy's students are motivated.
   e. Sandy uses reinforcements and recognition.
   f. In Sandy's class every student is a winner.
   g. Sandy and her students are enthusiastic.
   h. The students in Sandy's rooms are of average ability.
   i. At times, most students in this room seem to have been overachievers.

SUGGESTED READINGS

Adamson, C. (1985). Creativity in the classroom (brainstorming). *Pointer*, *29*, 11–15.

Bergmann, S. (1987). Teaching middle-schoolers decision-making skills. *Education Digest*, *52*, 48–50.

Clark, W. H., Jr. (1986). Some thoughts on teaching creativity. *Journal of Aesthetic Education*, *20*, 27–36.

Davis, G. A. (1987). What to teach when you teach creativity. *Gifted Children Today*, *10*, 7–10.

De Bono, E. (1986). A technique for teaching creative thinking (CORT program). *Momentum*, *17*, 17–19.

Isaksen, S. G., & Parnes, S. J. (1985). Curriculum planning for creative thinking and problem solving. *Journal of Creative Behavior*, *19*, 1–29.

Strahan, D. B. (1986). Guided thinking: A research-based approach to effective middle grades instruction. *The Clearing House*, *60*, 149–155.

Why Do We Have to Learn this Stuff?

THE COMMUNITY

Cedar City is a small southern town of about 13,000 residents. A city it's not. One flashing caution light and its CITY LIMITS signs are the only visible evidence that it has to support its name. The reaction of most visitors is that Cedar City is a good place to be *from*. Others are even less kind, pointing out that the only thing that prevents Cedar City from being a hick town is that it isn't even a town.

But the residents of Cedar City are not bothered by outsiders' comments. They have a satisfied feeling about their town. Their open, trusting nature is often completely misunderstood by visitors. For example, the town's one real estate office has a sitting area for guests. Each day, during the noon hour, the town's only realtor, Mr. John Grimes, leaves the outside door open. In the waiting area, Mr. Grimes places a sign on his desk that reads, "I have gone home for lunch. Please pour yourself a cup of coffee and make yourself at home. If you are in a hurry you can use my phone to call me at 304–8626. Otherwise, I'll be back at about 1:30."

There is a rumor that until recently the mayor of Cedar City took a daily stroll from one end of main street to the other looking for strangers. When he saw one, he introduced himself and offerred to buy the visitor a cup of coffee. Whenever a stranger accepted his offer, the mayor provided not only a cup of coffee but also a very persuasive sales pitch on the qualities of Cedar City.

THE SCHOOL DISTRICT

Both the size and the casual appearance of Cedar City are in many ways deceptive. While visitors might imagine that the inhabitants sit on their porches and watch the grass grow, the fact is that the residents of Cedar City are very active. Cedar City is the home of Cedar Mills, which makes some of the nation's highest-quality linens and bedding. The founders of Cedar Mills have lived in the town for several generations, and they love their community and display this love by supporting their schools. Cedar City Junior High may be the only junior high school in the country with separate gymnasiums for boys and girls, two completely furnished exercise rooms, an indoor Olympic-size swimming pool, and a twenty-lane bowling alley.

The well-equipped gyms and exercise rooms lead one to conclude that the resident philanthropists are sports enthusiasts, but the support given for athletics is actually small compared to that given to Cedar City schools' academic programs. Especially impressive is the direct financial support that the owners of Cedar Mills give annually to elevate the salaries of all teachers in the Cedar City schools.

THE TEACHER

The school district's attractive salary schedule and the well-equipped science laboratory are two features that attracted Mr. Paul Stinson to teach eighth-grade science at Cedar City Junior High. The twenty-three-year-old Mr. Stinson's wit and charm are two of the qualities that attracted his employers to Mr. Stinson. Whatever the reasons for hiring Mr. Stinson, the eighth-graders, like the rest of the residents, are glad that he chose the system and that it chose him.

Mr. Stinson is a thorough planner, but all of his plans have a unique element. Into each lesson he plans humor. Last Monday was the first day of study for his gifted section of eighth-grade science in a unit on geology. Before Mr. Stinson began introducing the unit, a thin, freckle-faced, red-haired boy named Everett Barnes shouted from the doorway as he entered the room. "Mr. Stinson, why do we have to study this stuff?" Mr. Stinson acted stunned and hurt. As their teacher quietly pouted, the students began to laugh. When all the students had taken their seats, Mr. Stinson slowly and carefully moved to the front of the class and sat down on a tall stool.

To begin the lesson, Mr. Stinson held up three rocks. "There are three types of rocks: sedimentary, metamorphic, and ignorant—I mean igneous." He paused for a moment and continued. "Actually," he explained, "all rocks are ignorant." He then told the class a story about rocks. The students sat entranced. (Incidentally, in his biological science class he uses the same approach when he introduces a unit on reptiles. "There are three deadly, poisonous snakes in this state, so you don't have to worry about them because

I killed three poisonous snakes last year." Then he introduces the three types of local poisonous snakes. Although his humor is perhaps a little corny, his caring attitude causes his jokes to succeed with students of all ability levels.)

Next, Mr. Stinson introduced the scientific method. He explained that Sir Francis Bacon was first to develop the scientific method. "You remember Bacon; he's the one who discovered the process of preserving bacon by freezing it in the snow." Again, the students laughed. He then told them that refrigeration was one of Sir Francis Bacon's many discoveries. By the end of the period, Mr. Stinson carefully tied the major concepts introduced during the hour into a tightly structured lesson.

During most of the lessons, the students were willing to sit back and enjoy their teacher's witty comments, and Mr. Stinson usually enjoyed most of the wit of his bright students. But occasionally a few students seemed to want to take over the class, or would turn to each other and make insulting comments. Whenever Mr. Stinson noticed this behavior developing he would slowly climb down from his stool and walk over to the overactive students and stand nearby, continuing the lesson without commenting on the misbehavior. The infractions usually ceased. If not, he often placed his hand on a misbehaving student's shoulder without saying anything to the student. No words were needed; the students got the message. Sometimes when the chattering got too loud Mr. Stinson lowered his voice. Those students who were interested in hearing him shushed their noisy classmates.

Mr. Stinson frequently spent his planning periods watching the students practice basketball or cheerleading. Each spring he planned field trips for all of his students. Each winter he planned a science fair. This endeavor alone required him to give up several weekends, as he always helped students from his lower-ability sections identify project topics, and he always offered to help students plan and develop their projects.

When students volunteered to develop projects for the fair, Mr. Stinson was careful to find something good to say about the projects. This is the same way he related to students in class when they turned in projects or test papers; he always wrote positive comments on each student's paper.

It was clear to everyone that Mr. Stinson enjoyed teaching and believed that every student in his classes was capable of learning whatever topic was being studied. In fact, he used his humor to motivate his students; while they enjoyed his entertaining dialogue, they also learned the central concepts of each lesson before they realized what had happened.

THE INCIDENT

Mr. Stinson's students frequently reciprocated his warmth and enthusiasm by challenging him to participate in a variety of activities at school including tennis matches, billiards, and basketball. It was the first day of spring and a party was planned around the outdoor city pool. A group of students asked him to attend the social function. Their level of enthusiasm was very convincing, but Mr. Stinson wondered whether he should maintain some distance between himself and his students. To accept the invitation might be going too far; yet to refuse might upset his students. He wondered if he himself had caused a problem by being too close to his students. Perhaps he should remove the humor from his future lessons.

THE CHALLENGE: If you were in Mr. Stinson's place what you do?

KEY ISSUES FOR STUDY:

1. Mr. Stinson was prepared for the one perpetual question that all teachers hear: Why do we have to study this stuff? In answering this question, Mr. Stinson used his strong rapport with students. Is this wise, or is a teacher obligated to use logic to answer student's questions?

2. How much do you believe that Mr. Stinson's wide acceptance by his students resulted from his interactions with them outside the classroom? On what evidence do you base your answer?

3. Cedar City has a friendly, small-town atmosphere. To what extent should teachers' out-of-school contacts with students be affected by the nature of the community?

4. Mr. Stinson effectively used humor when teaching his lessons, but he did this at the expense of getting off the subject. For example, he directed the students' attention away from geology long enough to give some personal information about Sir Francis Bacon's life. In light of the current emphasis on achievement, do you believe that a teacher is justified in taking this liberty? Why? Why not?

5. A much simpler and faster answer to the question about the subject's importance is that the students will be held accountable for it on their next test or they will need to understand this content in order to pursue the more advanced concepts next year. What are your reactions to these two explanations?

6. The question "Why do we have to study this stuff?" implies a certain amount of apathy for the subject. To what degree, if any, do you believe teachers are responsible for motivating their students?

7. Mr. Stinson frequently used nonverbal communications as part of his classroom management strategies. Specifically, he used this method to control student disrespect for their classmates. Do you think this is necessary? Explain your answer.

8. What evidence is there in this case that Mr. Stinson uses reinforcement in his classes? Do you think this affects the students' perception of Mr. Stinson? If so, how?

9. Recent research shows that teachers' levels of confidence in their students' abilities affect students' achievement level. What can you say about Mr. Stinson's level of confidence in the ability of his students? Can you give specific evidence to support this statement?

10. The upcoming event for which Mr. Stinson received the invitation from his students is described as a social event and it is being held at city pool rather than on school grounds. Should this affect his decision to accept or reject the invitation? Why or Why not?

SUGGESTED READINGS

Baughman, M. D. (1974). *Baughman's handbook of humor in education.* West Nyack, NY: Parker Publishing.

Cornett, C. E. (1986). *Learning through Laughter: Humor in the Classroom.* Phi Delta Kappa Fastback No. 241. Bloomington, IN: Phi Delta Kappa, International.

Discussion. (1985). What's the funniest thing that's happened in your class this year? *English Journal, 74,* 43–46.

Green, J. L. (1987). Meno's motivation: Foundations of learning. *The Educational Forum, 51*(2), 151–165.

Lasley, Thomas J. (1987). Classroom management: A developmental view. *The Educational Forum, 51*(3), 285–298.

Otten, N. (1986). Punchlines as paradigms. *English Journal, 25,* 51–53.

Slesnick, T. (1986). That's funny? *Classroom Computer Learning, 6,* 70–71.

Zeigler, V., Boardman, G., & Thomas, M.D. (1985). Humor, leadership, and school climate. *The Clearing House, 58,* 346–348.

CASE 26

Diagnosing a Reading Problem

Simpson City Elementary School is the pride of a quiet farming community in northern Oklahoma. Part of the Carroll County Schools, it is the newest building in the school system. It has been in operation for two years, housing two sections per grade level in grades kindergarten through six. Besides being the newest facility in the district, it is the only new building in a small town that is obviously fighting to survive.

When Diane Mason graduated from the local state college, she jumped at the opportunity to teach in Simpson City, which is twelve miles from her home in Medford, the county seat of Carroll County. In fact, the principal of the school, Jim Barrows, is married to Diane's older sister. In college, Diane was an average student who exhibited a great deal of enthusiasm for teaching. She was involved in student activities, and her extroverted personality served her well.

Diane is assigned to a third-grade class of twenty-eight students. The school year is now at the midpoint, and she has gotten to know each of her students quite well. Not unexpectedly, the children exhibit a wide range of abilities. Using some of the techniques acquired in her teacher education program, she has been able to do a reasonably good job of grouping the children for instructional purposes. All but one of the students progressed academically during the first four months of school. The exception, Peter West, seemed to be going nowhere.

The gray January skies presented a gloomy background for the start of school this Monday morning. Diane had devoted some time over the weekend to preparing special materials for Peter. She was anxious to put her

118

creativity to work. Giving the other students a reading assignment, she took Peter to a corner of the room to work on phonemes. She hoped that this type of exercise would increase his word-attack skills.

"Peter, we are going to work on sounds today. I want you to pay attention. I'm going to make a sound and you indicate which letters make these sounds by pointing to them on this chart. This will help you develop relationships between sounds and symbols," Miss Mason instructed.

Peter nodded that he understood. The first sound Miss Mason presented was the humming of the letter *m*. Peter thought for a moment and pointed to the *n*.

"Peter, that's wrong. It was the *m* not the *n*," she said in frustration. "Now listen more closely, I'm going to give you another one."

This time she made the sound for a *ch*. Peter pointed to the *sh*.

"Are you really trying or are you just being stubborn?" the teacher inquired. Before the boy could answer, she said, "Let's try one more."

The result was the same. Peter pointed to the wrong letter. Miss Mason took a deep breath and decided it was time to try something else. When Peter fails at assigned tasks he becomes quite restless. His attention span shortens, and he appears to be embarrassed by his lack of achievement. He starts looking around the room and wiggling in his chair.

"Peter, we are going to try something else. You know the alphabet because I've seen you write it. Now I'm going to give you a list of ten words. I'm going to sound them out for you first. Look at the first letter in each word. We are going to arrange the words alphabetically. Let me give you an example. Here are three words, *cat*, *mouse*, and *dog*. Since *cat* starts with *c* and since *c* appears in the alphabet before the first letters of the other two words, it would be placed first. Do you understand?" she asked.

Again Peter nodded that he did. Miss Mason handed him a list of ten words. She pointed to each as she presented the word orally. After reading all ten words, she asked Peter to concentrate on the first letter in each word. She sounded the letter again phonetically. Then she asked Peter to order them alphabetically. After struggling for ten minutes, he was unable to complete the task successfully.

"You know what your problem is, Peter? You don't listen," Miss Mason declared. "This is not a difficult assignment. You should have been able to do it before you got out of the first grade. If you're not going to listen to instructions, I'm not going to waste a lot of time with you."

Diane was totally frustrated. She knew that Peter was not stupid. He could, and did, do some things very well. He was probably better than anyone else in the class at solving puzzles. He was creative; he had imagination; he was not a behavior problem; but he just refused to learn to read. Diane was convinced of two things. First, Peter had to learn word-attack skills. Second, he wasn't going to learn anything if his listening skills did not improve. What she didn't know was what to try next.

THE CHALLENGE: Put yourself in Diane Mason's place. What would you do next?

KEY ISSUES FOR STUDY:

1. Is it possible that Diane's diagnosis regarding Peter's listening skills is correct? Explain your answer.
2. Do you agree with Diane's conclusion that Peter will never learn to read unless he develops word-attack skills? Why or why not?
3. Identify potential resources Diane could turn to for assistance in dealing with this problem.
4. Assess the importance of each of the following factors with regard to dealing with Peter's problem:
   a. the geographic location of the school
   b. the experience of the teacher
   c. the familial relationship of the principal and the teacher
   d. the size of the class
   e. Peter's skill in solving puzzles
   f. Peter's creativity
5. Does Peter's behavior suggest any problem other than difficulty with listening skills? Explain your answer.
6. Is it a good idea for the teacher to work with Peter alone while all the other children are doing assignments? Explain your answer.
7. Evaluate Diane's dependence upon a phonics approach with Peter.
8. Discuss Diane's general attitude in working with Peter. Do you think she was too abrupt? Why or why not?

SUGGESTED READINGS

Armstrong, T. (1985). How real are learning disabilities? *Learning, 14(2)*, 44–47.

Bender, W. (1985). Differences between learning disabled and non-learning-disabled children in temperament and behavior. *Learning Disabilities Quarterly, 8*, 11–18.

Brophy, J. E. (1983). Classroom organization and management. *Elementary School Journal, 83*, 264–285.

Candler, A. (1983). The differences among children with learning problems. *Education, 104*, 219–223.

Friedrich, D., Fuller, G., & Devis, D. (1984). Learning disability: Fact and fiction. *Journal of Learning Disabilities, 17*, 205–209.

Phipps, P. (1984). Regular classroom teachers look at LD classrooms. *Academic Therapy, 19*, 599–605.

Slate, J., & Saudargas, R. (1986). Differences in learning disabled and average students' classroom behaviors. *Learning Disabilities Quarterly, 9*, 61–67.

Smith, C. (1985). Learning disabilities: Past and present. *Journal of Learning Disabilities, 18*, 513–517.

Tarver, S. (1986). Cognitive behavior modification, direct instruction and holistic approaches to the education of students with learning disabilities. *Journal of Learning Disabilities*, *19*, 368–375.

Will, M. (1986). Educating children with learning problems: A shared responsibility. *Exceptional Children*, *52*, 411–415. (Also see September 1987 issue, pp. 66–68.)

Zahorik, J. (1986). Let's be realistic about flexibility in teaching. *Educational Leadership*, *44*, 50–51.

CASE 27

Covering for a Student's Absence

Katie Nelson, a student at Mason County High School, spent the summer studying at the Interlocken Music Camp. During the final competition she won the Beethoven Medal, signifying the top performance in the piano division. Her ten years of study with harpsichord and piano instructor Hardin Watson had paid off.

As a result of her performance she was eligible for the Medallion Competition in Chicago in January—a prelude to a possible concert at Carnegie Hall. As she planned her practice session, she hoped to schedule two hours at school each day—one hour during study hall and another hour during a scheduled music class. She knew she would need to rehearse four hours each weekday to master Aram Khachaturian's "Toccata" and Ernest Bloch's "Sea Poems."

Within Mason County, Katie became an instant celebrity. A front page headline in the *Mason Bulletin* the morning after her performance read: Katie Nelson May Play Carnegie. Two local radio stations aired her Interlocken performance, and she was interviewed on a television program. There was a parade in her hometown of Anchorville, where most all of the 1,400 citizens lined Main Street to cheer her upon her return.

When she started school she was hounded for autographs by students. Many of the teachers took time in class to have Katie share the highlights of summer camp, her winning performance, and how she might get to Carnegie Hall. It took her three days to get into the school routine.

Because of the attention given to her the first week of school, Katie had not been able to get in four hours of practice each day. She had hoped to practice two hours each morning—second and third periods. She had English first period, a study hall second, music third, then lunch, followed by home economics, mathematics, history, and science.

Berlin Malenski, her third-period music teacher, had been accommodating, allowing her to practice on Monday, Wednesday, and Friday. But he insisted she participate in the class two days a week. Under ordinary circumstances, Katie would have been able to use study hall time to practice. However, because she had to spend time practicing each night, Katie needed study hall to prepare for her afternoon classes. Although she was talented as a musician, school work never came easy for Katie. Through careful organization, hard work, and an outgoing personality, she plodded through school as an average student.

Gradually, Katie began to skip her home-economics class. She missed one class during the second week of school. She did not tell anyone where she was going, but went to one of the three soundproof practice rooms in the music wing of the school. Before the bell rang at the end of the period, Mr. Malenski, as he made a habit of doing, peered through the window to each of the practice rooms. When he saw Katie practicing, he knocked on the door and entered, saying: "Katie, what are you doing here?"

"Practicing," she responded.

"I know that," Mr. Malenski said, chuckling. "Did someone write a pass for you?"

"No." Katie said.

"You know you can get in trouble for missing a class without a written excuse," Mr. Malenski said.

"Why don't you write one for me?" Katie asked.

Mr. Malenski hesitated, then said: "Look, I don't approve of your missing one of your classes to practice. What class is it?"

"Just an elective, home ec," Katie said. "You know...cooking, food, family stuff."

"Who is your teacher?" Mr. Malenski asked.

"Ms. Wells. She's new this year."

Rhonda Wells had come to Mason County High School with superlative recommendations. She was a member of Kappa Delta Pi, graduated magna cum laude, had served as both president and vice-president of the Student Education Association, and had been recognized as an "Outstanding Future Teacher" by the state Association of Colleges of Teacher Education. She sees her strengths as an in-depth understanding of the home economics field as well as planning, organization, and discipline. She believes that most problems in the classroom arise because a lack of careful lesson planning and implementation. She stands firm on rules.

During the first day of classes Ms. Wells had clearly stated orally and in writing (in course outlines) what she expected of students. She discussed attendance, noting that she would deduct points for each absence. She described the level of quality expected in homework, projects, and tests, indicating how each would be evaluated.

Ms. Wells is eager to share her love of home economics with her students. "There's so much information that can be applied on a daily basis and can help improve the quality of students' lives," Ms. Wells believed. She entered the year hoping her enthusiasm for the subject would quickly become contagious.

With some reluctance Mr. Malenski wrote a note, indicating he endorsed Katie's absence because of "preparation for a critically important musical event."

Berlin Malenski is considered "a soft touch" by students who have musical talent and hope to pursue a musical career beyond high school. He identifies with these students, for he once aspired to work as a professional musician. His talent fell short. After several auditions, he realized he would never attain his dream.

Mr. Malenski is an ardent advocate for a strong music curriculum. He defends the music curriculum as important as physics, chemistry, English, or any other subject. Since coming to Mason County, he added "History of Music" and "Music Theory" courses to the curriculum. He has volunteered for and served on districtwide curriculum committees "to protect the integrity of the fine arts."

To Mr. Malenski, music is his life. He had not married because he believed that the time needed to build a quality music program precluded building other relationships. In a sense, he was married to his job. Most weeknights and weekends he worked with music groups at school and in the community. Routinely, he devoted ten to fourteen hours each day to his work. For this effort he had received state and national recognition.

That night Mr. Malenski received a phone call from Merriem Nelson, Katie's mother. Mrs. Nelson expressed her appreciation of Mr. Malenski for having written the pass, and she noted that when Katie came home from school, she seemed relieved—more relaxed. She shared how much pressure Katie felt—how demanding her piano instructor Hardin Watson was, how difficult schoolwork was, and how intense Katie was.

Mr. Malenki said he understood.

"I hope you really do," Mrs. Nelson said. "Please continue to provide support. You're the only teacher Katie can rely on."

Mr. Malenski felt good. It was nice getting a compliment from a parent.

On Wednesday of the following week, Mr. Malenski made his routine check of the practice rooms and again discovered Katie rehearsing. As before, he entered and asked, "Katie, did Ms. Wells approve your coming here to practice?"

"No." Katie said.

"Then why are you here?" Mr. Malenski asked.

Looking tired and near tears, Katie pleaded with Mr. Malenski. "I just don't have enough time. I feel too much pressure. You've got to help me!"

"Why don't we go talk to Ms. Wells. I'm sure she will understand," Mr. Malenski said.

"Please! No!" Katie shouted. "She'll punish me!"

Feeling Katie's distress, Mr. Malenski wrote her a pass to excuse her from Ms. Wells's class that day. He had mixed feelings about his actions, yet he had promised Katie he would not talk with Ms. Wells.

Twice the next week Mr. Malenski wrote excuses for Katie, making four times she had missed the home-economics class. Each time Mr. Malenski received a phone call from Mrs. Nelson expressing appreciation for his support.

"I'm a patient person," Rhonda Wells thought to herself as she placed an X in her grade book to record Katie's fourth absence. As a new teacher at Mason High School, she had assumed that the notes from Mr. Malenski were legitimate. Now she felt that regardless of what reasons Mr. Malenski might offer for Katie's absence, her continual absences were not acceptable.

She realized the status accorded Katie. Without doubt she was the most notable figure in the county. She also knew that Mr. Malenski was highly respected in the school and the community. Under his leadership the Mason High School orchestra and the Mason Civic Band had received state and regional recognition.

"My home-economics class is important too," Ms. Wells thought aloud. "I'm going to do something about this situation."

THE CHALLENGE: What should Ms. Wells do?

KEY ISSUES FOR STUDY:

1. How would you resolve Katie Nelson's continual absences?
2. What would you say to Katie?
3. If you were Ms. Wells, would you talk to Mr. Malenski? If so, what would you say?
4. What additional information would you like in order to make a decision?
5. What information in this case is irrelevant for making a decision?

SUGGESTED READINGS

Ban, J. (1987). Discipline literacy for parents: An imperative for the eighties. *NASSP Bulletin*, *71*, 111–115.

Blase, J. (1987). The politics of teaching: The teacher-parent relationship and the dynamics of diplomacy. *Journal of Teacher Education*, *38*, 53–60.

Calabrese, R. (1985). Communication is the key to good discipline. *NASSP Bulletin*, *69*, 109–110.

Combs, A. W. (1985). Achieving self-discipline: Some basic principles. *Theory into Practice*, *24*, 260–263.

Cornell, N. (1986). Encouraging responsibility—A discipline plan that works. *Learning*, *15(2)*, 46–49.

Curwin, R. L., & Mendlar, A. N. (1984). High standards for effective discipline. *Educational Leadership*, *41*, 75–76.

Dixon, M. (1983). Nine ways kids need you and how you can manage to meet those needs. *Instructor*, *93*, 74–75.

Hutslar, S., Litcher, J., & Knight, P. (1985). What motivates students to learn. *NASSP Bulletin*, *69*, 94–97.

Kasambira, K. (1984). To motivate students or not to motivate—is that the question? *American Secondary Education*, *13*(3), 6–10.

Kreidler, W. J. (1984). How well do you resolve conflict? *Instructor*, *93*, 30–33.

Lamb, K. (1985). In quest of excellence. *Teacher Education Quarterly*, *12*(2), 10–13.

Loekavitch, J. (1986). Motivating the unmotivated student. *Techniques*, *2*(4), 317–321.

Maggs R. (1986). The team approach for more effective discipline. *NASSP Bulletin*, *70*, 123–124.

Saver, R., & Chamberlain, D. (1985). Follow these six steps and learn to manage student misbehavior. *American School Board Journal*, *172*, 421.

CASE 28

Can I Borrow That Lesson?

Paul Santini, a veteran teacher of sixteen years, had grown tired of school opening. He found the initial faculty meeting "a waste of time." He took a book, paper, and pen to the meeting and took a seat in the back of the room.

The year before he had begun sharing feelings of being burned out. "I'm tired of fighting lethargic, disinterested youth," he had thought. In recent years he spent much less time revising lessons, depending largely on materials he had used previously. On occasion he tried to cajole other teachers into giving him lesson plans and accompanying materials and tests. At the same time, he began to experience more serious discipline problems.

Privately, other teachers noticed a dramatic change in Paul Santini's personality. He was more abrasive, quick to react to conflict, disorganized, uncompromising, opinionated, and sarcastic. He seldom had a kind word for anyone.

Despite his attitude Paul was still highly respected for his knowledge. He had attempted to revive his enthusiasm for teaching by attending summer seminars sponsored by the National Endowment for the Humanities. These experiences had refueled his interest in literature but had little effect on his desire to teach. In many ways spending the preceding summer at Cornell, his alma mater, had renewed a long-time dream of teaching English at a university, where he believed he would have more mature, scholarly students.

In contrast to Paul Santini, Arlene Winston, also a veteran of more than a decade of teaching, eagerly awaited the beginning of another school year. Each summer she reviewed activities used the preceding year and sought ways to improve them. Once a week she met with three other English teachers from area schools to explore trends in teaching English. Also, they discussed a novel each had read the preceding week. Arlene Winston found these informal professional development sessions inspiring.

During the summer, she also enjoyed tutoring students in grammar and composition. She met with six students twice a week in her home for three hours to work. She charged $6 per hour per student. She felt tutoring students who were experiencing failure helped sharpen her teaching skills.

The remainder of her summer, including an entire week preceding the opening of school, she devoted to her husband and two teenage daughters. The week before school the family vacationed at a new location each year. On weekends the family took day trips to sites of historical and cultural interest. Transporting the girls to softball and soccer practice, 4-H, and the library occupied much of her remaining time.

During the academic year, Arlene enrolled in a college course each term. "I don't need the credits. I just find learning vigorous," she had explained to her husband. Over the years, since completing the master's degree in English education, she had taken courses in anthropology, philosophy, sociology, Chinese, and art. She believed these experiences enriched her teaching.

Carlos Burton, entering his first year of teaching, was the most enthusiastic of the three English teachers. Since childhood he had dreamed of having his own classroom and students. With his father and grandmother as teachers he felt he was carrying forward a family tradition. He fondly remembered the hours his grandmother had "played school" with him. She had converted a small area in the basement of her house as a classroom and furnished it with refinished oak desks, a chalkboard, and a teacher's oak desk and chair. She stored boxes there filled with discarded materials—paper, wooden blocks, worn textbooks, used workbooks, packages of crayons, containers of paints, pens, pencils, and brushes. An American flag and nineteenth-century player piano were prized objects.

Carlos's father was a chemistry teacher and baseball and cross-country coach. As a child, his father took him to all the games and meets. He helped to chalk-line the baseball diamond, drag the field, and put down the bases. He served as an honorary bat boy. He set markers on the cross-country course. He had enjoyed the busy schedule, and he had valued the opportunity to meet so many people.

He carried on his interest in athletics when he attended Lincoln State, a black college. He had excelled in track and field and baseball. He had been an active member of the speech and theater clubs. Routinely, he made the Dean's List. In the college yearbook he had been labeled "Most Likely to Succeed."

Carlos Burton's strengths are his speaking and dramatic talent, knowledge of traditional ethnic literature, belief in his ability to inspire young people, and dedication to long hours of preparation. He believes that "you get out of life what you put into it" and is convinced that his peers should work as hard as he does.

The three English teachers walked from the department faculty meeting and headed toward their classrooms.

"Really, Carlos, I want to know. Why did you choose to come to teach in Walnut Hills schools," Paul Santini asked.

"The schools have a superb academic reputation. I'm within a two-hour drive of my parents. And the 'perks' are outstanding," Carlos Burton replied.

"I couldn't believe the incentive package the business and industry council put together," Arlene Winston added. "A month's free rent at Shadow Lane Apartments. Discounts at selected restaurants. Help with moving expenses."

"And a starting salary of $23,000 doesn't hurt, does it?" Paul interrupted.

"No, it doesn't," Carlos said crisply.

"And breaking tradition as the first black English teacher at Centennial probably gives you pride," Paul continued.

"I can't believe you," Arlene interjected with surprise.

"Hey, no offense," Paul shot back sharply.

"That had not entered my mind," Carlos responded.

"Well, it's good to have you here," Paul said, as he turned to enter his classroom. "We'll be seeing a lot of one another."

"Goodbye," Carlos responded.

"See you tomorrow, Paul," Arlene said.

As they walked toward adjoining rooms, Arlene told Carlos, "Paul is relatively harmless. He means well, but he isn't very sensitive. He's not noted for his tact."

"That's okay," Carlos responded. "He doesn't bother me."

"I saw from the schedule that each of us has at least one section of literature," Arlene remarked, making an effort to steer the conversation away from the tension she felt.

"Yes, I have two literature classes—first and third periods," Carlos said.

"Mine are both in the afternoon," Arlene replied. "And Paul has a section first period, too, I think."

"I believe he said he did," Carlos responded.

"See you tomorrow, Carlos," Arlene said, holding out her hand to shake his.

"Welcome to Centennial. Let me know how I can help."

"Thank you, Arlene," Carlos said.

The two teachers entered their classrooms and worked on getting their rooms and materials organized for the first day of classes. About an hour later Carlos left. As he walked down the hall, he was met by Paul, who had also decided to depart.

"All set for tomorrow?" Paul asked.

"Pretty much," Carlos replied. "I'm going to give each period my best shot. I have some unique lessons planned for the week."

"I'd like to see what you're planning. We both have a section of American literature during first period," Paut noted. "Maybe we can get together and share some ideas."

"Sounds good to me," Carlos replied.

As they left the building, each teacher went his separate way. As Carlos neared his car, he spotted Arlene Winston motioning to him.

"Carlos, I need to talk to you," she shouted, as she walked hurriedly toward him.

As she neared, she lowered her voice and said, "I overheard your conversation with Paul. I want to warn you. Paul Santini has a history of conning teachers into sharing lesson plans. He gets what he wants, but never gives anything in return."

"Thanks, but I don't want to pass judgment. I've only been here a few days. I'll have to form my own opinions about people," Carlos said.

"Well, I wanted to share this information with you. You'll find out what I mean," she said.

"I know you have my best interests at heart," Carlos remarked. "But I hope you understand why I can't pass judgment on people, before I really know them."

"Sure, Carlos, I understand," Arlene replied.

The next day Carlos's first-period class was a smashing success. He had planned a lesson to get the students interested in poetry by building on their love of music. He began the class by telling the students he wanted to introduce them to two contemporary poets. At first there were groans. But when a song by Simon and Garfunkel began playing on the phonograph, the students became attentive. When the song "Richard Cory" was finished, Carlos turned off the phonograph and awaited the students' reactions.

"That's not poetry," a student suggested immediately. "That's folk music. My mom and dad listen to that stuff all the time."

"Mine, too," another student offered. "That was Simon and Garfunkel."

"Before we decide that what you heard was not poetry, I want you to read the following handout," said Carlos, as he distributed a copy of Edwin Arlington Robinson's poem "Richard Cory."

As students were reading the poem, one said, "Looks like the lyrics to the song." Several other students agreed aloud.

After the students had all read the handout, Carlos said, "I want to play the song again. As I do, pay careful attention to the handout."

At the conclusion of the song, he asked, "What did you notice between the lyrics in the song and the words in the handout?"

Several hands went up. He looked at his seating chart and said, "Julie, did you see any differences?"

"Some of the words were different. But not many. The lyrics and the words are nearly identical," Julie responded.

Carlos continued the discussion, explaining that "Richard Cory" was a poem written by the renowned American poet Edwin Arlington Robinson.

Comparisons were made between the poem and the song in terms of word choice, sentence structure, tone, rhythm, and meaning. Enticing the students to study poetry through music had worked. The class period had gone quickly. As they left the room, the students were buzzing. They were excited about the class and looked forward to returning the next day.

Later in the afternoon Paul Santini stopped Carlos in the hallway and said, "Congratulations!"

"For what?" Carlos Burton asked.

"Students from your two American literature classes this morning are already tabbing you as 'Teacher of the Year,' he said, chuckling. "They told me about your use of music to introduce them to poetry."

"What are the chances today of my getting the plaque?" Carlos joked. "I don't want to risk my popularity for too long."

"Seriously though, getting them listening to a song and then springing the poem on them was an act of genius," Paul Santini continued. "What are the chances I could try out your lesson in my first-period class tomorrow?"

"The entire lesson?" Carlos Burton asked.

"Yes. You could give me the materials after school and coach me on what to do. That shouldn't take more than ten minutes. I'll share some of my stuff with you later on. What do you say?" Paul Santini asked.

THE CHALLENGE: You are Carlos. Will you share your lesson plan and materials?

KEY ISSUES FOR STUDY:

1. Would you give your lesson plan and materials to Paul Santini? Explain your answer.
2. What ethical issues are raised?
3. What concerns emerge in regard to professional practice?
4. What issues are raised in regard to social relations among teachers?
5. What additional information would be helpful in making a decision in this case?
6. What information in this case is irrelevant?

SUGGESTED READINGS

Applegate, J. H., Flora, V. R., & Lasley, T. J. (1980). New teachers seek support: Some people are supportive and others aren't. *Educational Leadership*, *38*(1), 74–76.

Feezel, J. (1986). Elements of teacher communication competence. *Communication Education*, *35*, 254–268.

Hawthorne, R. K. (1986). The professional teacher's dilemma: Balancing autonomy and obligation. *Educational Leadership*, *44*(2), 34–35.

Howlett, P. (1987). Speak out...and up...and early...and well. *Thrust, 16,* 18–19.

Katzner, L. I. (1986). Teaching from an ethical sensibility. *American Secondary Education, 15*(2), 6–8.

Kohlberg, L. (1970). *Moral education.* Cambridge, MA: Harvard University Press.

Lanier, J., & Cusick, P. (1985). An oath for professional educators. *Phi Delta Kappan, 66,* 711–712.

Saltis, J. (1986). Teaching professional ethics. *Journal of Teacher Education, 37*(3), 2–4.

Tennyson, W., & Strom, S. (1986). Beyond professional standards: Developing responsibleness. *Journal of Counseling and Development, 64,* 298–302.

Yeazell, M. (1986). The neglected competency—moral sensibility. *Contemporary Education, 57*(4), 173–175.

CASE 29

Dealing with Children's Transition to School

Los Altos is a large urban center with a highly diverse population of approximately 700,000 people. Tourism, banking, and finance are the primary employers in this year-round, warm-weather port city. Nearly 65 percent of the city's employed citizens work in service-related occupations. Because of its location on the West Coast, in recent years the city has received a large influx of refugees from Southeast Asia.

Twelve percent of the population of Los Altos are Asian, 3 percent are Arab, 27 percent are black, 48 percent are Hispanic, and 10 percent are white. Twenty-seven different languages, including dialects, are spoken in this metropolitan area. Most of the neighborhoods in Los Altos are racially and ethnically segregated. There is little integrated housing. Within the last seventeen years the racial breakdown of the city has gone from 73 percent Caucasian and 27 percent minority population to 10 percent Caucasian and 90 percent minority.

Los Altos Unified School District is a K–12 district and has the state's fourth largest enrollment. As the community has changed, the schools have been affected by white flight to private schools and to suburban school districts. At the same time, among minority groups many high socioeconomic status citizens have also chosen to send their children to private schools or have moved to the suburbs. In response, a federal court judge has placed the district in a court-mandated, countywide desegregation plan, which is a "tri-ethnic" plan that lumps both Asians and Caucasians into a "majority" classification. All other groups are considered minorities. Given the size of the Hispanic and black populations, each comprises the other segments of the 'tri-ethnic" plan. The judge has ruled that every effort must be made to provide racial balance in the schools. A balance of 60 percent to 40 percent minority/majority or 60 percent to 40 percent majority/minority is required.

The school district is divided into three geographic areas. Area A is the northern part of the district, comprised mostly of Caucasian and Asian residents, with a sprinkling of high socioeconomic status minority inhabitants. People who live in this area are employed primarily in professional positions. Area B is the east-central and southeast part of the district. For the past decade it has been largely populated by Hispanics. More recently, emigrants from Southeast Asia have tilted the racial and ethnic balance. Most of the citizens are factory workers and service employees. Area C is the western third of Los Altos Unified School District. Blacks, largely employed in blue-collar jobs, occupy this region of the city.

Each of the three areas has a superintendent, a curriculum specialist, a personnel and a financial affairs officer, and a health, safety, and transportation officer. The district superintendent, Larry Brock, has served in this position for fourteen years. When he became superintendent, he surrounded himself with loyal administrators hired "from the outside." Each subordinate administrator in the district has autonomy in making decisions. Dr. Brock prides himself on being an effective delegator.

Los Altos Central Elementary School, a K–6 school, was erected in 1928. It is the oldest school building left in the city. At least 12 percent of the students who begin the year at Central Elementary leave before the end of the school year. About 3 percent of these departing students return the following year, because their parents are seasonal farm workers who come back to the neighborhood when their work is done. There are 360 students and 23 faculty and staff members. Two sections of classes are usually offered at each grade level, except kindergarten, which has one section only. Nearly 25 percent of the students speak a primary language other than English.

Mr. Frederick Alvarez, the twenty-seven-year-old principal, has a bachelor's degree in elementary education and a master's degree in educational administration. He was born and has lived all of his life in Los Altos. He is known as a strict disciplinarian and a hard-line follower of school policies and procedures. He is extremely loyal to the Area B superintendent, who is also Hispanic and a lifetime resident of Los Altos. Most of the teachers at Central Elementary are black and Hispanic. Four of the twenty-three faculty and staff members are Caucasian and five are Asian-American.

Donna Liu is one of the Asian-American teachers on the staff. For all but the first six years of her life she has resided with her parents and two brothers in an integrated neighborhood in Los Altos. He parents own and operate a restaurant in Echo Park, the Los Altos neighborhood in which they live. Both of her brothers are older. One works in the family business; the other is an accountant with a computer company.

Ms. Liu is a new graduate of Los Altos State University. For most of her life she intended to work in the family business. While she completed a precollege curriculum in high school, she matriculated at Los Altos University, declaring a major in economics and a minor in marketing in the School of Business. After one semester, she became disenchanted with business. Because not all of her course work would transfer to the elementary school teaching credential, she took courses during two summers "to catch up."

Donna Liu takes pride in her creative ability. As a college student, she participated in a folk dance group, exhibited a showing of watercolors, and performed in the university orchestra. She also ran cross-country on the track team. She approached her first year of teaching with confidence and excitement.

Her position at Central Elementary serves as a fifth year—an internship year—in which she is being supervised by Naydean Todd, her mentor teacher. The internship year is a relatively new requirement passed recently by the state legislature. Every prospective teacher must undergo this probationary year. The salary is the same as formerly paid to beginning teachers. At the end of the year, her principal—Fred Alvarez—must make a recommendation to the department of education concerning certification for Ms. Liu. His options are to recommend for immediate certification, for a second year of internship work, or for dismissal from the school.

Mr. Alvarez has taken the position that he will make a recommendation, but will rely heavily on input from experienced teachers who serve as mentors in his school. Mrs. Naydean Todd has been at Central Elementary for twenty-three years. She came to the school as one of the first black teachers in a group of four hired as a part of the district's aggressive affirmative action plan. Like Ms. Liu, she has resided in Los Altos most of her life. She moved to the city from Birmingham, Alabama, when she was three years old. She also attended Los Altos State, when the institution was still a college. For her mentoring work, Mrs. Todd receives fifty minutes of released time one day each week. This schedule is designed to allow her to observe Ms. Liu.

Mrs. Todd is considered a "pillar" of the school. Not only has she taught longer than any other teacher there but she has also twice been named "Teacher of the Year" in the school district. She is known as a straightforward, no-nonsense, demanding teacher. She is impatient, expecting other teachers to be as hard-working and as skilled as she.

Ms. Liu has two sections of kindergarten—one in the morning and one in the afternoon. She has twenty-six children in the morning and twenty-three in the afternoon. The morning class consists of seven white, ten black, six Hispanic, and three Asian children. Nearly one-third of the youngsters come from single-family homes and live in low-income, government-subsidized housing. Another third come from blue-color families. The remainder have parents who hold professional positions. A wide range of social maturity and academic abilities is reflected in the class. The afternoon class is much less balanced, with two white, eighteen black, two Hispanic, and one Asian child enrolled. More than half of the children come from welfare homes. Only three of the students come from homes where the parents occupy white-collar jobs. Most of the children are of low ability.

The first few weeks have been hectic for Ms. Liu. Organization of the classroom has not been a problem. Two days after commencement she was at Central Elementary developing learning centers, making colorful bulletin boards, and preparing daily schedules for activities. With pride she created hats of different shapes and colors, each with one child's name on it, to be used as name tags the first few days of school. She organized the closet space in the classroom, identifying each child's space with a picture of a zoo animal. Although the janitors had cleaned her room before she arrived, Ms. Liu had coaxed her brothers to help polish the floors, scrub the walls and windows, and clean the desks and chalkboards on a weekend before the start of school.

She prepared five learning centers and two general areas in the classroom: one for small-group reading and one for "quiet time."

Each of the learning centers has a focus. One is stocked with various plastic and wooden manipulatives (puzzles, building blocks, figures). A second center serves as a science area. Jars with insects and small animals, plants, and rocks adorn the table. A third center contains art materials—paper of different sizes, shapes, colors, and textures. Crayons of every conceivable color occupy two shoe boxes. Word cards, large letters of the alphabet, large-lined paper, and pencils are stacked on a fourth table. A record player, records, and "dress-up" clothes are neatly organized on a fifth table.

The "quiet time" area has an old, worn couch, an oversized stuffed chair, several colorful bean bag pillows, and a fluffy throw rug. Adjacent to this area is the small-group reading area where another throw rug was fitted in the midst of several book shelves jammed tightly with simple readers and picture books.

Ms. Liu has been provided with a paid aide for both sections of her class. Mrs. Valerie Munoz, the mother of two children enrolled in the upper grades at Central Elementary, is assigned to the morning class. Martha Spinnel, a sixty-two-year-old widow and grandmother, is assigned to the afternoon class. Ms. Liu had visited briefly with both aides before the start of school, but because they were not required to work before the first day of classes, she was not sure how she would work with them. Nonetheless, she was pleased to have their assistance.

The first day of school had been trying. In the first section of kindergarten fifteen children came to class. Ms. Liu could not account for the other eleven on her roster. Of the fifteen children who arrived, two of the children spoke no English. Several cried when their mother or father left. A few of the children wore dirty, worn clothes and appeared hungry. The suspicion was verified during the snack period, when several children kept asking for more food or tried to take food from other children's desks. A couple of shouting matches and a scuffle with fists had resulted. Through the morning Ms. Liu felt as if she were riding a high-speed, nonstop Ferris wheel. Several children constantly vied for her attention. She found that the ability level of the children varied immensely, from youngsters who could not recognize shapes and colors, tie their shoes, zip their pants, or put on their jackets to others who not only knew shapes and colors but also could print their names, phone numbers, and a few words. Three of the children could even read some of the simple materials she had prepared for later in the year.

The afternoon went in the similar way, although it was not as tense. A greater number of students listed on her roster had arrived, but she faced the same problems with highly varied ability levels. Unlike the morning, when no one had become ill, during the afternoon two children vomited. At the end of the day Ms. Liu was exhausted. She had assumed that getting through the first day was the test and that the coming days would get better.

They did not. Each day seemed to mirror the first. Attendance during each session was spotty. She spent time each night trying to contact parents, with mixed success. Several of the children had no phone in the home. In most instances when she did reach a parent, relative, or sibling on the phone, there was an excuse for her student's absence: The child had been ill; the parents had overslept; the car had broken down. Because she could not reach each child's parent, she decided to visit the homes of children who were absent. This effort had similar results. In some cases the address she was given was incorrect. In one instance there was an empty lot at the address to which she had driven. In several cases the parents appeared embarrassed when she arrived. In only a few instances did she appear to be welcome.

The aides had not been as helpful as she had hoped. Mrs. Munoz had trouble following directions. Although she was expected to spend most of her time in clerical work, Mrs. Munoz preferred interacting with the children. Ms. Liu spent an inordinate amount of time each day redirecting Mrs. Munoz. In contrast, Martha Spinnel did precisely what she was asked to do. However, she was slow and careless. Ms. Liu found herself correcting Mrs. Spinnel's mistakes. In some ways having an aide in the class was like having an additional child in the room.

On Friday morning of the first week Mrs. Todd was scheduled to visit Ms. Liu in her classroom. Midway through the morning, Mrs. Todd arrived. Immediately, as Mrs. Todd entered, several of the children scrambled around her and tugged at her dress. Ms. Liu, with some struggle, managed to get the children back to their learning centers. Mrs. Todd took a seat in the corner in the back of the room. With a notepad and pen in hand she recorded the following notes:

- Lacks confidence, seems unsure of self.
- Variety of centers provides interest (at some centers children do not seem to have a purpose).

- Aide appears to jump from activity to activity. Doesn't stay with or follow through with an activity.
- Children appear to like Ms. Liu. They are friendly toward her, vie for her attention (some by acting out in negative ways).
- Has difficulty maintaining overall order.
- Room is neat, tidy, and colorful.

After fifty minutes of observing, Mrs. Todd got up to leave. On her way out she stopped and said to Ms. Liu, "Let's have lunch together as planned. I'll meet you back here in your room at noon. We'll go over my notes at that time."

"Okay," Ms. Liu said. "See you then."

From the time Mrs. Todd left until the morning class was dismissed, troubled thoughts flashed across Ms. Liu's mind. All of them pointed to the fact that she didn't think the class went well during the observation. As she had packed a lunch that day, she waited for Mrs. Todd to arrive from the cafeteria. Until Mrs. Todd arrived she prepared the class for the afternoon session. At two minutes past noon Mrs. Todd, carrying a tray of food, tapped at the door. Ms. Liu hurried to the door and opened it.

"Thank you for taking time from your lunch hour to visit with me," Ms. Liu greeted.

"No problem. I think it's probably the best time for both of us," Mrs. Todd observed.

After pushing stacks of children's books aside, they sat down together at one of the tables used for an open reading center. "Let's go over my notes," Mrs. Todd began.

Over the weekend Ms. Liu thought about the kindergarten classes.

THE CHALLENGE: You are Ms. Liu. What would you determine to be the most critical problem to be solved?

KEY ISSUES FOR STUDY:

1. What behaviors are exhibited by the children that contribute to problems in the kindergarten classes?
2. In what ways might Ms. Liu's behavior and inexperience add to classroom difficulties?
3. How might the organization of content affect classroom problems?
4. What role do the children's parents play?
5. Has the behavior of the aides contributed to classroom difficulties?
6. What is known about the characteristics—motivation, attitudes, work habits, etc.—of the children that may be a contributing factor?

7. What additional information would be helpful in analyzing problems in the kindergarten classes?
8. What information is irrelevant for analyzing problems in the classes?

SUGGESTED READINGS

Bredekamp, S. (Ed.). (1986). *Developmentally appropriate practice*. Washington, DC: National Association for the Education of Young Children.

Curtis, S. (1987). New views on movement development and implications for curriculum in early childhood education. In C. Seefeldt (Ed.), *Early childhood curriculum: A review of current research* (pp. 257–270). New York: Teachers College Press.

Elkind, D. (1986). Formal education and early childhood education: An essential difference. *Phi Delta Kappan, 67*, 631–636.

Feeney, S., & Chun, R. (1985). Research in review: Effective teachers of young children. *Young Children, 41*(1), 47–52.

Gehrke, N., & Kay, R. (1984). The socialization of beginning teachers through mentor-protege relationships. *Journal of Teacher Education, 35*(3), 21–24.

Genishi, C. (1987). Acquiring oral language and communicative competence. In C. Seefeldt (Ed.). *Early childhood curriculum: A review of current research* (pp. 75–106). New York: Teachers College Press.

Goffin, S., & Tull, C. (1985). Problem solving: Encouraging active learning. *Young Children, 40*(3), 28–32.

Gottfried, A. (1983). Intrinsic motivation in young children. *Young Children, 39*(1), 64–73.

Honig, A. S. (1985). Research in review. Compliance, control, and discipline (Parts 1 & 2). *Young Children, 40*(2), 50–58; *40*(3), 47–52.

Kamii, C. (1985). Leading primary education toward excellence: Beyond worksheets and drill. *Young Children, 40*(6), 3–9.

Katz, L. (1980). Mothering and teaching: Some significant distinctions. In L. Datz (Ed.), *Current topics in early childhood education* (Vol. 3, pp. 47–64). Norwood, NJ: Ablex.

Novatis, B. (1986). Maintaining a positive attitude. *Early Years, 17*, 63–65.

Prawat, R., & Nickerson, J. (1985). The relationship between teacher thought and action and student affective outcomes. *Elementary School Journal, 85*, 529–540.

Shelby, A. (1985). Is your teaching style frustrating your students? *Learning, 14(3)*, 46–48.

Spodek, B. (1985). *Teaching in the early years* (3rd ed.). Englewood Cliffs, NJ: Prentice-Hall.

Walsh, E. (1984). Effective teaching: Is it mostly common sense? *Principal, 64*, 30–32.

Wellman, H. M. (1982). The foundations of knowledge: Concept development in the young child. In S. G. Moore & C. R. Cooper (Eds.), *The young child: Reviews of research* (Vol. 3, pp. 115–134). Washington, DC: National Association for the Education of Young Children.

Willert, M., & Kamii, C. (1985). Reading in kindergarten: Direct versus indirect teaching. *Young Children*, *40*(4), 3–9.

Young child at school, the. (1986). *Educational Leadership*, *44*, 3–12.

Zahn, G. (1986). Cooperative learning and classroom climate. *Journal of School Psychology*, *24*, 351–362.

CASE 30

The Problems with Packaged Planning

MAYNARD BUCKLES NAMED BASKETBALL COACH AT KHS, read the headline in the Klutchville newspaper in early July.

Hiring a first-year teacher to be head basketball coach is rare; but then again, Klutchville is not an average high school. Located in rural area of a mid-Atlantic state, it is a very small secondary school. With an enrollment of only 110 pupils in four grades, the school has fended off numerous consolidation attempts initiated by neighboring districts.

The principal, Edison Jones, would have preferred a more mature individual to head up the school's primary athletic program. But such individuals simply do not stand in line for a job that requires teaching three different classes and coaching in a program where only three victories have been recorded in the last four years. In a school as small as Klutchville, the talent is limited.

If nothing else, Maynard Buckles is a daredevil. He's the sort of fellow who always volunteers to get hypnotized at a magic show. Unfortunately, his enthusiasm for adventure was not matched by his performance as a student at Haslow College. School was a genuine struggle for Maynard. In fact, were it not for his basketball talents in high school and the athletic scholarship those talents produced, he probably would never have been granted admission to Haslow.

After three semesters in prelaw, Maynard decided that he had better concentrate on becoming a coach—and, yes, a teacher. He decided to major in physical education and minor in government (only because he had taken several courses in government already). His basketball career at Haslow ended when he shattered his knee in a motorcycle accident in the summer

141

between his second and third years of college. The school, however, honored his scholarship, and he helped Coach Day with the team. It took a fifth year (at Maynard's own expense), but he finally graduated from Haslow.

Maynard's teaching assignment at Klutchville High School includes three classes of physical education, one class of health education, and one class of civics. The civics assignment is his greatest challenge.

The civics class has seventeen students—sophomores, juniors, and even two seniors. With the help of Roger Piper, the athletic director at KHS and an industrial education teacher, Maynard mapped out a strategy to cope with this assignment.

"The key to keeping your head above water," Piper told Maynard, "is to plan all your lessons before basketball season. There's a teacher's manual for the civics textbook. Map out what you're going to do every day. Even the tests are included. After that, it's pretty automatic. You won't be bogged down when you have to spend time with basketball."

This advice was given on August 10, and the very next day Maynard started planning every lesson for the year. By the time school opened on September 2 he had a file folder for every civics class to be held between September and June.

For each class Maynard had his dittos, his notes, his outlines, and his objectives. Like a well-oiled machine, he presented his lecture and then the next day's assignment.

Mr. Jones, the principal, was impressed. One day in early October he commented, "Maynard, I hear good things about you from my daughter, who is one of your students. She says that you come to civics class well prepared. I like that in a new teacher."

Maynard diligently stuck to his scheduled lessons. On several occasions, students would raise their hands in class and ask him to go over something he had presented the previous day. Maynard wasn't going to fall victim to that old trick. He remembered how he had tried the same "stall tactic" on some of his professors at Haslow College. When such requests were made, Maynard simply told the students to talk to each other after class. If they didn't understand something from the previous day's lesson, it wasn't his fault.

Maynard also had strict policies about homework. He assigned homework every day, but it was never the type that required students to submit the product—usually it was a reading assignment or the completion of ditto sheets that Maynard never reviewed.

Basketball practice started in mid-October and KHS played its first game on November 12. Maynard knew that basketball would take the majority of his time and energy, but he hadn't expected it to be such a drain on his emotional well-being. By February 1, the team had one win and fourteen losses.

The basketball team's record was not the only factor that darkened February 1. After Maynard's last class, which was during fifth period, he went to the gym to change clothes for basketball practice. The door to the coach's office burst open and there stood Principal Jones, his face as red as an over-ripe tomato.

"Buckles, what the hell happened in your civics class?" he demanded. "I just saw your semester grades—two B's, three C's; seven D's; and five F's. And my daughter, Melanie, you gave her a D. She's never had a D before!"

"Gee, Mr. Jones, I thought you told me I was doing a grand job. You said that you liked the way I prepared for class," Maynard asserted nervously.

"Forget that. What about these grades? How can so many students do so poorly?" he fumed.

"Mr. Jones, I used the tests that come with the teacher's manual. They're multiple choice. The teacher's manual even tells you which grade to assign for the number answered correctly. If students don't get it, that's their fault. I told them we would only have one exam each semester and that exam would determine their grades. I was just being fair," explained Maynard.

As Edison Jones stood there, his face turned an even deeper red and beads of perspiration now became visible on his forehead. "Well, I'll tell you what, Mr. Know-it-all," he finally managed to say. "You're going to change these grades to be fair to the kids. You're going to do it and be quiet about it. Every grade should be raised at least one level. You understand?"

The principal turned on his heels and slammed the door so hard as he left that it loosened the hinges.

THE CHALLENGE: Analyze Maynard's teaching strategy. What would you do if you found yourself in this predicament?

KEY ISSUES FOR STUDY:

1. Did Mr. Piper give Maynard good advice about preparing for his civics class? Why or why not?
2. Assess Maynard's strategy for evaluating pupil progress.
3. What are the advantages and disadvantages of Maynard doing what the principal demands?
4. Did Mr. Jones, the principal, contribute to the problem of low grades in the civics class?
5. In what ways did the coaching assignment affect Maynard's performance as a teacher?
6. Discuss the repercussions of establishing a precedent by changing grades.
7. Discuss the legal and ethical ramifications of changing student grades once they are given.
8. Based upon the facts in this case, can you determine if Maynard was properly prepared by the Haslow College faculty to teach civics?
9. Why do you think Maynard decided to base the semester grade entirely on the outcome of one examination?

10. Can the practice of determining grades solely on the basis of an examination ever be justified? Why? Why not?

11. In reality, what is the educational philosophy of Klutchville High School?

12. Does the fact that the class included sophomores, juniors, and seniors have any bearing on this case?

13. Analyze Maynard's policy regarding homework.

14. Assume that the students in Maynard's class received predominately A's and B's instead of D's and F's. Do you think his teaching/grading methods would have been questioned?

15. Should a beginning teacher's grades conform to the general level of grades issued by the other teachers? Why or why not?

SUGGESTED READINGS

Adams, T., Goodlad, J., & Hay, L. (1985–86). Students must be active participants in learning. *Today's Education*, pp. 8–9. (Special edition of *NEA Today*.)

Chiarelott, L. (1986). Competence and artistry in teaching. *American Secondary Education*, *15*(1), 8–11.

Hassenpflug, A. (1986). Teacher-administrator cooperation—a necessity for the effective school. *NASSP Bulletin*, *70*, 38–41.

Koslofsky, N. (1984). Planning and behavior—two factors that determine teacher success. *NASSP Bulletin*, *68*, 101–104.

Kowalski, T., & Weaver, R. (1988). Characteristics of outstanding teachers. *Action in Teacher Education*, *10(2)*, 93–100.

McNeil, L. (1988). Contradictions of control: Administrators and teachers. *Phi Delta Kappan*, *69*(5), 333–339.

Raths, J, Wojtaszek-Healy, M., N Della-Piana, C. (1987). Grading problems: A matter of communication. *Journal of Educational Research*, *80*, 133–137.

Thomas, W. (1986). Grading—why are school policies necessary? What are the issues? *NASSP Bulletin*, *70*, 23–26.

Yinger, R. (1986). Balancing the art and technics of teaching: Renewing the profession. *NASSP Bulletin*, *70*(491), 75–80.

Zahorik, J. (1986). Let's be realisitic about flexibility in teaching. *Educational Leadership*, *44*(2), 50–51.

CASE 31

Preventing and Controlling Discipline Problems

THE SCHOOL AND COMMUNITY

Greenwood Elementary was the first school to offer a position to Josephina. The state's low salary base had driven most of the education majors to accept positions in neighboring states. But Josephina felt very lucky because Greenwood, in her words, is "an ideal community." Many would agree that regardless of the pay scale, the small town of Greenwood has much to offer its teachers. Its population of 50,000 is large enough to support its one excellent hospital and its nice shopping mall. Education is valued by Greenwood's residents, and teachers are considered important community leaders. The town is virtually free of traffic problems. A major city located only twenty miles away is an easy half-hour drive on the interstate. In the mid-1980s Greenwood Elementary was selected as a school of excellence. Its location and reputation attracted students from the upper-middle and lower-upper economic strata.

THE TEACHER

Josephina Gomez was one of the brightest students in her graduating class. Throughout her program she applied her abilities well, earning a 3.5 overall grade point average and a 3.7 grade point average in her teacher education courses. But Josephina's talents were shaded by her introverted personality. Her reluctance to speak out was often interpreted as a weakness; her peers often concluded that her unwillingness to express herself resulted from a weak knowledge base or from a general lack of ability. Adjectives used by her peers to describe Josephina included *shy*, *introverted*, *shallow*, and *weak*.

THE INCIDENT

The first few days had gone as uneventfully as Josephina had expected. She was excited over the opportunity to teach her favorite subject, language arts. But things could have gone a little more smoothly. For example, from the first day, as each lesson began, a few students ignored Josephina's request for silence. She decided to ignore their continuous chattering, hoping these few students would become interested in the lesson once they reached the writing activities; all students would then give their undivided attention, Josephina believed. But this did not occur. In fact, each day, as she stood at the front of the room introducing the day's lesson and giving pertinent information, the noise from the class became increasingly louder. Most student comments were unrelated to the content in the day's lesson. Now, at the end of the second week, the students had gotten so loud that other teachers had begun complaining, saying that Ms. Gomez's classes were so noisy that they were disturbing the other classes nearby.

As the first-period class got underway one morning, the inevitable happened. Bob Carter, who had recently devoted his time and energy to aggravating his teachers and his classmates, was diligently pursuing this new interest by christening his neighbors with new names. Keith Adams, a light-complexioned and light-haired fifteen-year-old, was the chosen target for today's verbal abuse. Keith did not appear to mind the comments; in fact, he seemed to be completely ignoring them as Bob referred to him as "white-out," "liquid paper," "chalk head," and "Casper, the Friendly Ghost." Even though Keith ignored it, the name-calling worsened. But suddenly, without warning, Keith stood up and punched Bob squarely in the face. A burst of blood sprayed from Bob's nose. Seeing the blood frightened Bob and provided him with a surge of energy. He grabbed Keith and lifted him up, throwing him across a couple of desks. The other students watched with glee and welcomed the diversion from the otherwise boring lesson. Josephina was stunned by the violence. What could she do? She temporarily froze, watching in horror as Bob came crashing to the floor and Keith jumped squarely across him, pinning his shoulders to the floor.

Then Josephina found herself running across the room and pulling at Keith's collar as she shouted, "Stop it! Stop it!"

The swinging and kicking suddenly stopped and a pall of silence fell over the class. Now everyone in the room was eyeing the teacher, eager to see how she would respond. What should she do?

THE CHALLENGE: At some point in your career you may face such a crisis. Suppose you were Josephina. What would you do?

KEY ISSUES FOR STUDY:

1. Did the incident come without warning?
2. Josephina remained positioned in front of the room throughout the lesson. How does the teacher's location in the classroom affect discipline?
3. Although Josephina knew that some students were not paying attention, she chose to begin the lesson anyway. Is this wise?
4. This group had gotten so noisy that other teachers had started to complain. Should the teacher care what they think? Why or why not?
5. To what degree are these students' comments related to the content in the lesson?
6. Bob had been consciously disturbing classmates for several days. How should this affect Josephina's reaction to the situation?
7. Josephina considered sending both students to the principal's office with a note for the principal to punish them. Do you think that the principal would welcome the opportunity to discipline the students? Why or why not?
8. Do you think that the principal might view Josephina's request as a symbol of weakness? Why or why not?
9. Suppose the teacher ordered the students to go to the principal's office, but they chose instead to go someplace where they could get hurt. Would the teacher be liable should they, indeed, get hurt?
10. Might other students interpret this as a weakness in Josephina or as an inability to discipline her own students?
11. Suppose that on their way to the principal's office the students decided to fight again. Should one of them get injured, would the teacher be legally liable?
12. Suppose that Josephina decided personally to escort both students to the principal's office. While out of her room, should some of the students become injured, would Josephina be held responsible for the welfare of the other students left behind in the classroom?
13. Suppose Josephina decided to send both students to their seats and resume class as though nothing happened. Do you believe that this would minimize the seriousness of student participation in dangerous and unacceptable behavior?
14. Might these students and their classmates interpret Josephina's decision to send the students to the principal's office as failure to know what should be done or perhaps even as fear of taking action to discipline students?
15. Do you believe the students might admire Josephina for her ability to return the class to normal?
16. Might Josephina's determination to continue with the lesson communicate to everyone that the lesson was more important to Josephina than any student's attempt to disrupt it?

17. The teacher could discuss this incident with the entire class. Do you think that the students might appreciate the opportunity to be involved in the resolution of the problem since this lesson was disrupted and they may think they deserve an explanation?
18. Is there evidence that it is time for the teacher to clarify the expectations that she holds for this class?
19. What other, perhaps better, alternatives might Josephina pursue to handle this problem and minimize the probability of its recurrence?

SUGGESTED READINGS

Boynton, P. (1985). A basic survival guide for new teachers. *The Clearing House, 59,* 101–103.

Fifer, F. L. (1986). Effective classroom management. *Academic Therapy, 21,* 401–410.

Helm, D. J. (1985). Success versus failure in the classroom. *Education, 105,* 369–397.

Henson, K. T. (1988). *Methods and strategies for teaching in secondary and middle schools* (Chapter 13: From discipline to self-discipline). White Plains, NY: Longman.

Long, C. K. (1987). Classroom management: Finding answers to a complex problem. *The Clearing House, 68,* 261–217.

McDaniel, T. R. (1986). A primer on classroom discipline: Principles old and new. *Phi Delta Kappan, 68,* 63–67.

Manning, M. L. (1986). Beginning the school year: 25 things to remember. *Southern Education, 121,* 300–301.

Perreshene, S. (1986). Management made easy. *Instructor, 96,* 70–71.

CASE 32

Censorship or Administrative Responsibility?

"I can't believe it. I can't believe it," Susan Raines, journalism teacher at Eastwood High School, mumbled aloud.

An empty feeling came to her stomach, and a tear slid down her cheek.

"I can't believe it!" she shrieked.

She pressed the "off" button on the remote control and the television screen went dark.

"Five to three. Incredible," she thought. "I've got to respond."

She went to her desk, pulled a yellow pad and a pen from the drawer, and sat down. An hour later she stopped writing, folded the letter, placed it in an envelope, addressed it, and put a stamp on it. Then she went to her car and drove to the post office. As she dropped the letter into the box, she said angrily, "You may think you can censor my kids, but you can't censor me!"

The next evening she leafed through the local newspaper, the *Eastwood City Press*. When she came to page 8 she exclaimed, "They printed it!"

Slowly, focusing on each word, she read her letter to the editor:

Congress shall make no law respecting the establishment of religion, or prohibiting the free exercise thereof; or abridging the freedom of speech or of the press; of the right of the people to peaceably assemble, and to petition the government for the redress of grievances.

I remember these words from my social studies class in my junior year of high school. My teacher stressed the importance of freedom of expression. In the same year I read *1984* and *Fahrenheit 451* and learned why my rights to free speech had to be protected. One of the most profound events of my life also occurred that year. My high school newspaper adviser got fired, largely because she allowed my friends and me to express our opinions in the student newspaper.

A few years later I became a journalism teacher. Ironically, I found myself in a painfully similar situation. My high school principal recommended nonrenewal of my contract, saying laughingly: "I can't believe you think the student newspaper is a real-life paper. It's an organ of the school to give a positive image—not a forum for student criticism."

That summer I was reinstated. The next year I had four journalism classes and nearly a hundred eager students. They worked hard to find interesting, sometimes controversial stories of concern to other students. They did research and conducted interviews. They wrote features and news, intent on being fair and accurate.

The Supreme Court case of *Hazelwood School District* v. *Kuhlmeier* upheld the principal's right of censorship of the student newspaper—in this case to prevent the publication of an article on student pregnancies and one on the effects of divorce on young people.

Now, after this decision, will my students be free to express their ideas? Will they be allowed to write about teenage pregnancy? Drug abuse? Suicide? An inadequate curriculum? Incompetent teaching? Unfair grading?

The Supreme Court has spoken. But only three justices have spoken for my students and me.

During the evening, several friends called, praising Susan for writing the letter. She felt somewhat redeemed. Having the letter published was cathartic. She slept comfortably.

When she arrived at work the next morning, Susan was met at the school entrance by Mary Reeves, the drama teacher at Eastwood High.

"Susan, hurry—you've got to check your mail," she said excitedly.

"Why?" Susan asked.

"Look at this," she responded, handing a memo to her. It read:

January 15, 1989.
To: Mrs. Reeves, Drama Teacher
From: Mr. Marlin Erlick
Re: Theater Performances
As of this date, before any play or other theatrical performance can be performed publicly, the script must be submitted to me for review by my administrative staff. This procedure is being implemented not to censor or obstruct student performance. It is being set in place to assure that selections appropriate for the public are performed.

"I was afraid this would happen," Susan said.

They walked hurriedly toward the main office. Susan went in, gathered her mail, and returned to the hall, where Mary was waiting.

"Looks like I got one too," Susan remarked waving a piece of paper. "Mr. Erlick wants to see the student newspaper before it goes to the printer."

Before the first bell rang, Susan and Mary learned that the choral director, the band instructor, the art teachers, and the librarian had received similar letters. As the two teachers parted to teach their first-period classes, Mary said, "We've got to get together and do something."

"What should we do?" Mary asked.

"You get in touch with Mr. Carter, Mrs. Grimes, and Ms. Keene. I'll talk to Ms. Bertrand and Mr. Munoz. Can we use your room? I'll have students in mine, working on the next issue of the paper," Susan said.

"I have the same problem. Students are rehearsing scenes for *Sweet Charity*. Mrs. Grimes is working with the musicians for the performance. Mr. Carter has his room tied up with the students practicing the vocal parts. And Bertrand and Munoz have students working on flats," Mary responded.

"That leaves Ms. Keene. Maybe we can use one of the conference rooms. I'll check on it. See you at lunch."

During the lunch period, Susan and Mary met again. Everything was set. The conference room was reserved. All the teachers had agreed to meet at 4 P.M.

"Was there any reluctance to meet?" Susan asked.

"None, the teachers see Erlick's memo as an insult to their professional judgment. Not surprising, is it?" Mary asked.

"No. How did Bill, Marla, and Ms. Keene respond?"

"Bill and Ms. Keene are fine. So is Marla. . .really. Bill's concerned about her, since this is her first year. But Marla believes as strongly in this as we do."

"I knew we could count on Ms. Keene," Susan said.

It was critical for the teachers to get the support of Ms. Keene, the librarian. No one remembered her ever being called by her first name. She was always called "Ms. Keene." She was known as the "Grand Lady of Eastwood," wears the finest clothes from Saks, Gucchi, Bloomingdale's, and Neiman-Marcus, and lives in an antique-stocked colonial house listed in the National Registry. She belongs to the Daughters of the American Revolution, does volunteer work at the Eastwood Hospital Auxiliary, and regularly attends the Main Street Presbyterian Church. She is as much a leader in the community as she is in the school.

"Her presence demands respect," Susan added.

"What do you think about Marla? Should we leave her out of this?" Mary asked.

"Look, a new teacher can't ride the fence. She has to sink or swim on her own. She's old enough to teach. She's old enough to make up her mind," Susan responded matter-of-factly.

"Do you really think she has much choice? Surely she feels pressure from us."

"It's her decision. We'll make that clear to her," Susan stated.

"And Bill?"

"I think he mentioned Marla as a way of projecting his own feelings of insecurity. He's not real strong."

"I don't understand. He has tenure. He's been here for eight years," Mary replied. "What's his problem?"

"He's taking heat. Replacing Carol Middleton has been tough. The choral groups have never won the awards or performed as superbly as when Carol was the director. He feels like he's being pressed to leave. He doesn't feel he gets the financial support or the best students. He thinks it's intentional," Susan said.

"Well, there's no problem with Carlos and Lisa. They're union advocates and they believe that the principal's edict on censorship is, at best, an item that must be negotiated. They want to file a grievance," Mary remarked.

At 4 P.M. Mary and Susan headed for the library conference room. The other teachers were seated at the table when they arrived.

Susan assumed leadership of the group. She first summarized the circumstances leading to the meeting, and then she said, "I believe we must do something. That's why I wanted us to meet."

THE CHALLENGE: What should the teachers do?

KEY ISSUES FOR STUDY:

1. What specific actions should the teachers take?
2. What reasons can you give in support of the actions recommended?
3. What are potential consequences of these actions?
4. What rights do the teachers have?
5. What rights do the students have?
6. What rights does the principal have?
7. Ultimately, in this case, whose rights are the most likely to be protected? Explain your answer.

SUGGESTED READINGS

Adams, J. (1986). Districts "jump the gun" on prior restraint rules. *Communication: Journalism Education Today, 19*(4), 19–20.

Bowen, J. (1985). Captive voices: What progress, change has occurred in 10 years? *Quill and Scroll, 59*(3), 14–16.

Burress, L., Katz, L., Melichar, D., & Small, R. (1985). Facets: My biggest worry about censorship. *English Journal, 74*(1), 22–25.

Donelson, K. (1987). Censorship: Heading off the attack. *Educational Horizons, 65*, 167–170.

Flygare, T. J. (1986a). Supreme court restricts damages for constitutional violations. *Phi Delta Kappan*, *68*(4), 246–248.

Flygare, T. J. (1986b). Teachers' First Amendment rights eroding. *Phi Delta Kappan*, *67*(5), 396–397.

Joyce, R. P. (1985). Constitutional protections of teachers and other public employees. *School Law Bulletin*, *16*(2), 6–12.

Jurenas, A. (1987). A delicate balance—a familiar dilemma. *American Secondary Education*, *16*(1), 28–30.

Lehr, F. (1985). Academic freedom: A guide to major court cases. *English Journal*, *74*(1), 42–44.

Menacker, J., & Pascarella, E. T. (1984). What attitudes do educators have about student and teacher civil rights? *Urban Education*, *19*(2), 115–124.

Merrill, M. (1987). Authors fight back: One community's experience. *Library Journal*, *112*, 55–56.

Nelson, J. L., & Stanley, W. B. (1985). Issues in social studies education. Academic freedom: 50 years standing still. *Social Education*, *49*(8), 662–664, 666.

Osborn, D. R. (1984). Confessions of a high school newspaper advisor. *English Journal*, *73*(6), 64–66.

Sendor, B. (1985). Fairness is the key to balancing your authority with teachers' academic freedom. *American School Board Journal*, *172*(11), 26, 48.

Splitt, D. A. (1987). School law. *Executive Educator*, *9*(1), 5.

Zirkel, P. A., & Gluckman, I. B. (1984). Educators's free speech: New developments. *NASSP Bulletin*, *68*(475), 127–130.

CASE 33

The Challenge of Grading

Binghamton City School District takes pride in its standards of educational excellence: Grades given should reflect the quality of work completed by the students. The following grading system is used:

A = superior
B = excellent
C = average
D = poor
F = failure

David Marks reread the grading policy published in *The Teachers Handbook: Binghamton City Schools*. He had also read through the twenty-seven test papers from his second-period advanced mathematics class once. Before he marked the test papers he wanted to be certain he was following procedures.

"Can't be too careful, especially with the gifted students," he thought to himself. "If I'm not precise, they'll challenge me. I want to be prepared."

There was no doubt in David's mind about the potential for challenge from his students. The twenty-eight juniors and seniors in his class were admitted into the highly selective colloquium "Mind Problems" on the basis of their carrying an overall GPA of 3.7 (on a 4.0 scale), an A grade in all high school math courses, and a 680 or better score on the mathematics section of the Scholastic Aptitude Test (SAT). In addition, the students had to have the written recommendation of two teachers attesting to their leadership potential.

For the remainder of the evening Mark graded the papers. For each paper he reviewed the process used to solve the ten problems on the test along with the students' answers. He assigned a maximum of 5 points to the process and 5 points to the answer for a total of 100 possible points.

After he had marked all the papers he made a list of the point totals. Beside the totals he noted how many students obtained each score. He put a line under 72, indicating 14 scores above and 14 scores below the line. He looked for "natural breaks" in the scores and put broken lines above 58, 64, 81, and 90. Next he put letter grades next to the scores within an area. Next to the score of 93 he put A. For scores 84–90 he put B; for 66–81 he put C; for 62–64 he put D; and for 52–58 he put F.

SCORES

93	II	A
90	I	
87	I	B
86	I	
84	I	
81	III	
79	II	
75	I	
72	I	C
70	II	
68	I	
67	I	
66	II	
64	I	
63	II	D
62	II	
58	I	
57	I	F
52	I	

Mr. Marks entered a letter grade on each paper, using his grading scale.

The next morning before the advanced mathematics class began he printed the number of A's, B's, C's, D's, and F's on the chalkboard.

2	A
4	B

13   C
 5   D
 3   F

He was proud of the care with which he had graded his first test. He wanted to show his class that he had high expectations and was well organized.

After the students arrived and the bell rang, he distributed the test papers, saying: "I want to begin class by going over the tests. Each time I give a test I'll return your tests the next day and review them so that you can learn from your mistakes."

He walked down each row and returned each student's paper. He had folded each paper in half, vertically, so that students could not easily see one another's score. Seating the students alphabetically made it efficient for returning papers. As he passed out the papers, he said, "I've put the number of students receiving A, B, C, D and F grades on the chalkboard so you can see how you did in comparison with the other students."

As he passed out the papers, students began grumbling.

"Quiet, please," Mr. Marks said. "We'll go over the test in a minute."

"I can't believe this," one student said aloud. "I've *never* received a B on a math test."

"Me neither," another student agreed.

Several students echoed displeasure about the grade marked on their papers.

As Mr. Marks went through the test the students challenged him on every item. But he had prepared carefully and had an answer for each challenge. He was pleased with the quickness of his responses.

"I survived the challenge," he thought. He recalled his methods professor saying that you can loosen things up later, but you've got to show them you are in charge at the beginning.

During the remainder of the period, he lectured on a new math concept. With ten minutes left he assigned twenty-five problems from the mathematics text and told the students they could begin working on the problems. Until the bell rang he walked around the room, working with students who requested help.

As the students left the room, they continued mumbling about the grades they had received on the test.

Before he went to the cafeteria for lunch, Mr. Marks stopped by the main office to check his mail. He found two phone messages. One was from Mrs. Jamerson and another was from Mrs. Scrivens. "Jamerson and Scrivens must be the mothers of Elaine Jamerson and Marvin Scrivens—students in my second-period class," he thought.

He took the phone messages and left the other papers behind. He decided he would call after lunch. He made a habit of avoiding discussion of school activities and problems during the forty-minute lunch period. Typically, he ate with two coaches and an English teacher. They talked about sports, movies, and automobiles.

He finished lunch a few minutes early and went to a private phone in the counseling office.

He called Mrs. Jamerson.

"Hello," she answered.

"Mrs. Jamerson?" Mr. Marks asked.

"Yes?" she responded.

"This is Mr. Marks. You called," he said.

"Mr. Marks, Elaine called me after your class and asked me to come and get her. When I picked her up, she burst into tears. She cried so hard when she got home that she cried herself to sleep. She said she was humiliated in your class."

"I don't understand," Mr. Marks said.

"Probably not. Elaine works very hard to compete in the honors classes. Math is not her strongest subject. But she's never received an F. How do you explain giving her an F?" Mrs. Jamerson asked.

"She had one of the lowest scores in the class," Mr. Marks responded. "I believe it was next to the lowest."

"Compared to what?" Mrs. Jamerson asked.

"What do you mean, compared to what?" Mr. Marks responded.

"These young people are the brightest in the school. There are no average students in your class. So how could you fail anyone?" she asked.

As Mr. Marks started to explain, Mrs. Jamerson interrupted. "I won't have my daughter treated this way!" she snapped angrily, and hung up.

Mr. Marks was stunned. When he took the job at Binghamton he had developed a set of "personal policies." One was not to embarrass or humiliate a student. Another was to return parents' calls promptly. He was troubled by the results in this class.

He dialed the other number. Mrs. Scrivens answered.

"Mrs. Scrivens, this is Mr. Marks," he blurted out before she could respond. "You called earlier. I suppose you wanted to talk about the second-period class."

"Yes," she responded. "Marvin has a 4.0 average. He has not had a low grade in anything since third grade. We plan for him to go to Harvard, Yale, or Stanford."

"I'm pleased that you have high hopes for Marvin, but what does this have to do with my class?" Mr. Marks asked.

"Well, the B that you gave Marvin on his paper today—do you really believe that the grade is indicative of his ability?" she asked.

"I'm not certain," Mr. Marks said. "This was just the first test. He did B work on this test."

"We can't risk jeopardizing Marvin's 4.0 average. We may have to have him removed from your class if you can't give some assurance that he will excel," Mrs. Scrivens remarked.

"I can't guarantee how he will finish the course. Like I said, this was just the first test," Mr. Marks stated.

"Well, we expect him to get all A's. I trust you'll do what you can to see that he does," Mrs. Scrivens stressed.

"Mrs. Scrivens, I'm sorry, but I must go now to my next class," Mr. Marks said. "I can assure you that I work hard to bring out the best from all my students."

"Well, thank you for calling."

"You're welcome," Mr. Marks concluded. "Goodbye."

Mr. Marks was upset. He had difficulty teaching the rest of the afternoon. After his last class, he went to see Martha Givens, chairperson of the mathematics department.

"Can I talk with you for a couple of minutes?" he asked.

"About your second-period class?" Mrs. Givens responded.

"How did you know?" Mr. Marks said in astonishment.

"I've had Elaine and Marvin in class. Mrs. Scrivens and Mrs. Jamerson both called me this morning during my planning period," she said. "I know all about it."

"I can't believe they called you," Mr. Marks said. "I didn't do anything wrong."

"It's a matter of judgment. Students in your advanced math class could take an easier class and be certain of getting an A to keep a high grade-point-average. But they didn't do that," Mrs. Givens said.

"I followed the school district policy in assigning grades. I was very careful in grading their papers," Mr. Marks added defensively. "Should I give everyone in the class A's and B's?"

"It's your class, Mr. Marks. You need to decide for yourself," Mrs. Givens concluded.

THE CHALLENGE: You are Mr. Marks. How will you approach the issue of grading?

KEY ISSUES FOR STUDY:

1. Should you continue grading tests the way you have begun or consider another approach? Explain your response.
2. What information in the case led you to your decision?
3. What additional information would you like to have in order to make a decision?
4. What influence on your decision should the district's published grading policy have?
5. To what extent should Mrs. Givens's view be considered?

6. What effect will the parents' remarks have on your decision?

7. What information in the case is irrelevant for making decisions?

SUGGESTED READINGS

Andrews, A. (1983). Grade inflation—how great? What are the concerns of parents, educators? *NASSP Bulletin, 67,* 81–88.

Baksh, I., & Martin, W. (1984). Teacher expectation and the student perspective. *Clearing House, 57,* 341–343.

Crowl, T. K. (1984). Grading behavior and teachers' need for social approval. *Education, 104,* 291–295.

Curwin, R. L., & Mendler, A. N. (1984). High standards for effective discipline. *Educational Leadership, 41,* 75–76.

Driscoll, M. P. (1986). The relationship between grading standards and achievement: A new perspective. *Journal of Research and Development in Education, 19,* 13–17.

McLaughlin, T. (1987). Ethical perception and student grading. *Momentum, 18,* 57.

Malehorn, H. (1984). Ten better measures than giving grades. *Clearing House, 57,* 256–257.

Meece, J. (1985). Teacher communication and student roles. *Educational Digest, 51,* 50–53.

Perrin, R. (1986). Are some grades worth more than others? *Clearing House, 59,* 200.

Pestello, F. (1987). The social construction of grades. *Teaching Sociology, 15,* 414–417.

Saville, A. (1983). Ability grouping and grading systems—what are the alternatives? *NASSP Bulletin, 67,* 80–82.

Thomas, W. C. (1986). Grading—why are school policies necessary? What are the issues? *NASSP Bulletin, 70,* 23–26.

CASE 34

Teacher Effectiveness: Unrealistic Expectations Produce Excessive Student Anxiety

THE COMMUNITY

Madisonville is a city of 100,000. As the home of one of the nation's space flight centers, great emphasis is placed on education. When the space industry first moved to the area some thirty years ago, Madisonville was a sleepy little town of less than 10,000 people. But the city planners were aware that attracting scientists, engineers, and mathematicians to the area would require first-rate schools. The rapid growth in population was paralleled by a rapid growth in size and quality of the schools. Salaries were increased significantly for several years until they were far above the rest of the state. Madisonville residents are justified in taking great pride in their school system.

THE SCHOOLS

Madisonville Senior High, which once housed grades seven through twelve, expanded so that the lower three grades were removed, leaving only grades ten through twelve. A new junior high, Madisonville Junior High School, was built on a campus adjacent to the high school. All of the new elementary schools that sprang up over the past thirty years have been established as first-rate schools equipped with the best faculty and facilities available anywhere. Almost all of the teachers in the area hold master's degrees, and several have doctorates in their teaching fields.

Oakwood Junior High is a rural school located about ten miles from Madisonville. When the students graduate from Oakwood they are bused to

Madisonville Senior High for grades ten through twelve. Most Madisonville High graduates go on to one of the state's two major research universities. In recent years an increasing number of Madisonville graduates have received scholarships at such institutions as Stanford, Harvard, and M.I.T. This is not surprising for a school whose students win top national recognition every year.

THE TEACHERS

Lyle King and Clay Rutledge grew up in the Oakwood community. Both attended one of the state's major research universities. Their high school friendship continued as they roomed together throughout their college years. Because both of them chose to major in mathematics, they were classmates in the majority of their courses. Both were excellent students and were always among the top performers in their classes. Neither had given much thought to the type of job they wanted; they just enjoyed math.

During their senior year, both Lyle and Clay decided they wanted to teach high school math. It seemed too late to change colleges so they finished their degrees and immediately entered a new fifth-year program. Although called the fifth-year program, nobody completed the program in just one academic year, but by going to school full-time during each summer preceding and following the academic year, both completed the program in sixteen months.

As they approached the end of their program, Lyle and Clay both applied for teaching positions at Madisonville Senior High, but they were told that unlike most schools in the state, which seemed to always have a shortage of math teachers, for years Madisonville had maintained a standing list of experienced applicants waiting for an opening. They were advised to submit their applications and get their names added to the waiting list.

They followed this advice, while continuing their search for local teaching positions. Lyle was offered the only vacancy at Madison Junior High. Clay was less fortunate, but was offered a one-year position at Oakwood Junior High, which he gladly accepted. During this one year, he would replace Mrs. Gail Wright, who had taken a pregnancy leave of absence.

THE INCIDENT

Although Clay had to settle for teaching at what he knew was a far less prestigious school than Madisonville, he was not worried. After all, by the end of the year, a position would probably open at Madisonville. But Clay was concerned with the fact that he would be teaching at the junior high level. His fifth-year program had provided rather extensive field experiences, but all of them—including student teaching—had been at the senior high level.

Clay found that teaching math to the students at Oakwood Junior High seemed a near impossible challenge. The age group was noisy, but as individuals, most students were nice. Clay wondered why he wasn't elated over this new assignment. As he pondered the situation he concluded that it was the paradoxical nature of this job that made it both frustrating yet, at the same time, somewhat satisfying. Some of his students were very serious-minded (college bound); others were completely apathetic. On one day the group would be serious, displaying mature behavior, but on the next day even the more serious students would behave as immature, irresponsible children. During some lessons, they accepted responsibility with little prodding, but for other lessons they had to be coddled and spoon-fed. Clay remembered reading about the paradoxical nature of adolescence. His methods text explained it as a perpetual dilemma. Adolescents strive to be accepted as adults, yet they are pressured by their peers to behave immaturely.

As the first six-week grading period ended, Clay saw that his previous concerns had been justified. Several students in his class did not do well at all. Some of the parents, unhappy with their children's grades, requested a meeting with him to discuss this situation. Following the meeting, they concluded that Clay was not as effective as Ms. Wright, and they expressed concern to the principal, Ms. Cole, who summoned Clay for a discussion.

Clay entered the Office feeling certain that some of the parents had expressed their concern to Ms. Cole. "Good morning, Mr. Rutledge. Thanks for coming. I think you know there's been some concern among some parents about the rate of progress of their children. I hope you understand that it's not unusual for these parents to express concern over academic matters. They know that competition is keen at Madisonville High and they want to be sure that their children are well prepared. Math is the one subject of greatest concern, since for many of our students it's a stumbling block for admission to and success in college."

"Ms. Cole, I understand and I am equally concerned about this problem. I explained each lesson thoroughly. Sometimes these students absorb the new content like sponges, and the next day they seem completely resistant and determined to learn nothing. I teach all lessons the same way. I lecture for the first half of the period, then I assign problems. I may grade papers while they're busy with their seat assignments but I always welcome questions. Oh, yes, and I always give homework assignments."

"How about objectives? Do you have objectives identified for each lesson? And do you share these objectives with the students?

"I usually tell them that they'll need to master this lesson in order to go on to the next one. During the first week, I held an orientation session with each class and at that time I told them how each lesson builds on the previous one and each year on the previous year. I also told them that if they get behind in this class they probably will never catch up. They need to know this so they'll understand how important it is to get all of their work done."

"I see, Ms. Cole nodded. "Some of the parents said that their major concern is that their children are developing attitudes of hopelessness. Have you done anything that might cause them to feel inadequate in your class?"

"I just try to be realistic with them. Some kids simply don't have the ability to do math. I think I have to be honest with them, so I tell them that some of them won't make it. To do otherwise would just cause more pain later on," Clay explained.

"I know that it's hard to please everyone, especially when you're temporarily filling in for someone. I don't expect you to be another Mrs. Wright. Just try to relieve some of the anxiety among your students, and I'm sure everything will be fine. Please let me know if I can assist you. Thanks for coming in."

As Clay left the office he wondered how he should begin correcting this problem. He thought, "I need a plan to achieve this goal."

THE CHALLENGE: Suppose you were Clay. What would you do?

KEY ISSUES FOR STUDY:

1. Clay has no real objectives for each lesson. To what degree do you believe this influences the students' feelings of inadequacy?
2. All of Clay's field experiences involved high school students, yet these students are junior high students. How might this affect their feelings of inadequacy?
3. These concerned parents have high expectations for their children. Knowing this, should Clay adjust his level of expectations accordingly?
4. Clay thinks he needs a plan to achieve the goal of getting these students to feel more capable. What steps might such a plan have?
5. Clay is being told by the principal that she does not expect him to be like Mrs. Wright, yet he is being compared to her by the parents. How should he respond to this?
6. Each section of Clay's classes contain both serious, college-bound students and apathetic students. What can he do to respond to these diverse groups?
7. Clay's position at Oakwood is a temporary, one-year assignment. Should this affect his reaction to his session with Ms. Cole? If so, how?
8. Clay has said that he lectures for half the period and then gives the students an assignment to do in the second half of the period. Could his teaching methods be contributing to the existing problem?

SUGGESTED READINGS

Hartman, D. (1986). What do teachers want? *Vocational Education Journal, 61,* 26–28.
Kerr, M. M., & Zigmond, N. (1986). What do high school teachers want? A study of expectations and standards. *Education and Treatment of Children, 9,* 239–249.

Novatis, B. (1986). Maintaining a positive attitude. *Early Years*, *17*, 63–65.
Red, C., & Shainline, E. (1987). Teachers reflect on change. *Educational Leadership*, *44*, 38–40.
Robinson, G. E., & Protheroe, N. (1986). The teachers speak out. *Principal*, *65*, 58–60.
Swanson, B. B., & Koonce, P. M. (1986). Teacher incentive: Is merit pay enough? *Action in Teacher Education*, *8*, 87–90.

CASE 35

Gifted Students— Gifted Teacher

Gerald Lassiter was an outstanding student in elementary school, high school, and college. In his sophomore year of high school he took the SATs and scored 1,370. He was salutatorian of his high school class. When he enrolled in a major state university on the Atlantic coast, he surprised everyone, including his parents, by deciding to become a social studies teacher. In large measure, this decision was sparked by Gerald's admiration for one of his high school teachers.

Two months prior to completing his final year of college, Gerald was selected by the School of Education faculty as the outstanding senior in teacher education. With a grade point average of 3.9 (4.0 = A), he also graduated magna cum laude. The director of laboratory experiences at the university placed Gerald in one of the best schools in the state for student teaching, Benton West High School. After only one week, the principal, Dr. Joe Bradovich, recommended Gerald for permanent employment. When the director of personnel actually presented him with a contract, Gerald did not have to think very long about the offer. He immediately accepted the position.

Benton is a progressive city of 200,000 residents located on the mid-Atlantic coast. Two Fortune-500 companies have their headquarters in Benton, and it is the home of one of the best-known teaching hospitals in the country. West High School, serving an affluent area of the city comprised almost entirely of new housing divisions, has an enrollment of 1,300 in grades nine through twelve. It has won numerous citations for excellence. Gerald realized that Benton offered the social and cultural advantages of a major city, and that West High School was a dream come true for a first-year teacher.

Dr. Bradovich told Gerald that his tentative assignment would include three sections of American history and two sections of civics. During the summer between graduation and the start of his teaching career, Gerald worked for his father, a painting contractor. In his spare time, he prepared for the professional challenges that awaited him on September 1.

When Gerald and his father returned home after a long day of painting a house in the hot August sun, his mother informed him that Dr. Bradovich had called.

"What did he want?" Gerald inquired.

"I don't know. He wants you to call him as soon as possible. He said to call collect. His number is written on the pad next to the phone in the den."

Gerald immediately dialed the number and reached his principal.

"Hello, Dr. Bradovich. This is Gerald Lassiter. My mom said you called today."

"Thanks for returning the call. I understand that you're getting a marvelous tan this summer while holding that paint brush. But you probably gathered that I didn't call to discuss your tan. I have to make a minor change in your teaching assignment. We just had a late resignation from Eleanor Moody. She taught our section of social studies for gifted and talented students. I would like to give that class to you. However, I don't want you to have three different assignments. So, I'm going to give you another section of American history and transfer your civics classes to someone else. You'll have four sections of history along with the gifted and talented class."

After a long pause, Gerald responded, "I'm a little uncomfortable with having to take the class for gifted and talented. I don't have any special preparation in that area."

"Don't worry," Dr. Bradovich assured. "We have a coordinator in the central office who will supply you with plenty of assistance. Her name is Dr. Turner. I'm going to have her send you some materials right now so you can look them over in the two remaining weeks before school starts. I have a great deal of confidence in you. After all, you're a gifted person yourself. I think this assignment will be challenging for you and for the students."

Gerald was unsure whether to be worried or honored by the decision of his new principal. In reality, he felt both. Using some materials forwarded to him by Dr. Turner and two books he purchased from the university bookstore, Gerald spent the last week before the start of school consuming every bit of information that he could find about teaching the gifted.

Benton is located 150 miles from Gerald's hometown. The move to his apartment took less than three hours. His first official act when he got situated in Benton was to contact Dr. Turner and arrange an appointment. During the meeting, Dr. Turner gave Gerald a box of materials including specific lesson plans for the first ten classes.

"I suggest that you try to follow these plans as closely as possible," she urged him. Not knowing what was in the lesson plans, Gerald simply nodded and left.

The first day of classes was exciting. Gerald was especially anxious to meet his third-period class—the advanced section in social studies for the gifted and talented. There were ten students in the class. All were seniors.

When Gerald introduced himself, one young man in the front row immediately inquired, "What happened to Mrs. Moody? She was supposed to teach this class."

"Mrs. Moody resigned three or four weeks ago and the class was assigned to me," Gerald responded.

One female student asked, "Weren't you here student-teaching last spring? I think my sister was in your American history class."

For the most part, the students were pleasant. Gerald immediately sensed, however, that competition among the group was intense. These were the ten brightest students he had ever encountered. Given these conditions, he was thankful that Dr. Turner had provided him with the materials. He concluded that he would need all the help he could get.

On the third day of class, Gerald was surprised to find Dr. Turner sitting in the room at the beginning of the period. "Don't mind me," she said. "I just want to observe."

Dr. Turner returned at least once a week for the next three weeks. She would sit silently and never provided Gerald any feedback following her visits. At first, he didn't mind, but now the visits were becoming troublesome. In large measure this was due to the fact that things were not going as well as Gerald had hoped. The students exhibited little enthusiasm. They were overtly complaining about the class being "too routine"; and they kept asking when they would be doing things independently. Gerald decided it was time to talk to Dr. Bradovich.

The appointment took place in the principal's office after school. Gerald started by providing a brief history of what had occurred in the class up to that point. He was candid about the student dissatisfaction.

"Dr. Bradovich, I'm convinced that these students want to work more independently. Dr. Turner's lesson plans, the ones she gave me and wants me to follow, are designed to have the entire class doing the same things."

"Hasn't she been visiting your class?" the principal inquired.

"Yes, very frequently. But I never get anything from her except more lesson plans. I really think these students want to compete academically against each other. I think they want to be turned loose on challenging projects."

"Well, she's the expert, Gerald," the principal responded. "She's pretty well respected in this school system."

"When I decided to be a teacher," Gerald stated, "I thought I would have the opportunity to use my talents to be creative. You know, that is pretty much true with regard to my American history classes. Yet the gifted and talented class seems to be very confining. At times I feel like I'm just a robot in class. In this instance, I think the students are correct. The class is too confining."

"Gerald, you have a long and probably successful career ahead of you. Be patient. Schools require certain levels of structure. We cannot afford to have teachers doing 'their own thing.' Dr. Turner's paid to provide advice, and that's what she's doing."

THE CHALLENGE: Analyze this situation. Do you think Gerald has been placed in an unfair position? What would you do if you were Gerald?

KEY ISSUES FOR STUDY:

1. Discuss the principal's decision to assign the gifted and talented class to Gerald. What criteria did the principal use in making this decision? Was this a wise decision? Explain your answer.
2. Is Gerald at a disadvantage because he is a first-year teacher? Why or why not?
3. Is Gerald at a disadvantage because he was not prepared to be a teacher of the gifted and talented? Why or why not?
4. Discuss the positive and negative ramifications of teachers being given lesson plans that they are directed to follow.
5. Is it possible that the students are simply rebelling because they resent being placed in a class with a first-year teacher? Explain your answer.
6. Is it likely that gifted and talented students really want to work independently and compete against each other? Explain your answer.
7. Gifted students are often stereotyped as "weird" or "misfits." Is this a fair description of most gifted students? Explain your answer.
8. What negative effects could this situation have on Gerald's behavior as a teacher?
9. Should teachers have significant degrees of freedom to apply their professional skills? Should first-year teachers have any less freedom than their more experienced peers? Explain your answer.
10. Discuss Dr. Turner's failure to provide feedback to Gerald after her classroom visitations.

SUGGESTED READINGS

Barrington, B. (1987). Curriculum-based programs for the gifted. *Education Digest*, *52*, 48–51.

Freedman, I. (1985). Unwrapping each student's special gifts. *NASSP Bulletin*, *69*, 125–126.

Kolloff, P. B., & Feldhusen, J. F. (1986). Seminar: An instructional approach for gifted students. *The Gifted Child Today*, *9(5)*, 2–7.

Kowalski, T., & Weaver, R. (1988). Characteristics of outstanding teachers. *Action in Teacher Education*, *10(2)*, 93–100.

Moffett, K. L., St. John, J., & Isken, J. A. (1987). Training and coaching beginning teachers: An antidote to reality shock. *Educational Leadership*, *44*, 34–36.

Renzulli, J. S. (1978). What makes giftedness? Reexamining a definition. *Phi Delta Kappan*, *60*, 180–184, 261.

Ricca, J. (1984). Learning styles and preferred instructional strategies of gifted students. *Gifted Child Quarterly*, *28*, 121–126.

Sawyer, R., & DeLong, R. (1986). A square deal for smart kids. *Principal*, *66*, 41–44.

Sosniak, L. (1987). Gifted eduation boondoggles: A few bad apples or a rotten bushel? *Phi Delta Kappan*, *68*, 535–538.

Summy, J. (1983). Gifted and talented program development: The teacher as change-agent. *Education*, *104*, 44–46.

CASE 36

Introducing New Programs Brings Resistance

THE COMMUNITY

Capitol City is itself a fake name but the city that it represents is real. In fact, it is one of our nation's oldest state capitals. Like many other state capitals, Capitol City is the home of a major university that has a well-known and well-respected college of education.

THE SCHOOL

During the 1970s the growth in population necessitated the building of a new high school. The enrollment of Capitol High School had reached well over 3,000, causing many problems. It had become clear that the obvious answer to the problem (adding temporary classrooms) was no longer a viable option. Temporary classrooms had been tacked on to the existing structure until the entire physical plant looked like a patchwork quilt. Expressed diplomatically, Capitol High had lost much of its original charm. Put bluntly, Capitol High had become ugly.

But continuous increases in enrollment at Capitol High had caused an emergency-type expansion that resulted in dysfunctional physical facilities. Some departments are located on three different levels. Some of the newer types of programs have never found a central location for their departments.

Obviously, a new high school was the only sensible long-term option. The school board finally acted. Bonds were drafted and plans were under way to build a new high school that would rival Capitol High in size. But the new Capitol High East would be different; it would be carefully planned. Each department would be housed in its own building, located strategically according to the nature of the department.

THE AMERICAN STUDIES PROGRAM

Ironically, while bringing the overdue needed relief to the other teachers, the teachers of history and American government were very concerned about moving into the new facilities. To these teachers a new building in a new location meant a loss in cultural heritage—a thread that runs deep throughout their courses. The teachers shared their concern with the chair of the secondary education department at the local university. Dr. Higgins, a social studies methods teacher and an expert in experiential education, has been on the local university faculty for the past twenty years. He has taught most of the Capitol High social studies teachers. As a former director of student teaching, Dr. Higgins has worked closely with Capitol High. When some of the Capitol High social studies teachers came to him for help, he rallied his own faculty and the Capitol High social studies faculty, and began holding planning meetings. The results were an experience-based (experiential) American Studies program. Like all experiential programs, this program was loaded with meaningful hands-on student activities. All concepts and objectives were clearly identified and each one had an activity that made its attainment easy. An old two-story, nineteenth-century jailhouse was acquired for the home of the American Studies program. The building had been sitting vacant and uninhabited, except for the legendary ghost of a prisoner who had hanged himself from a large hook that still remains in one of the second-story rooms near the head of the stairs. A large open area on the second story has been turned into a replica of a nineteenth-century courtroom, where mock elections are held and where mock court cases are tried. A large glassed-in case near the base of the stairs displays artifacts the students have taken from archaeological digs. During the city and county elections, students participate in planning and conducting the election, and after each election they continue helping by cleaning up the city, removing campaign posters and other postelection debris. Each year's program culminates with a trip to Washington, D.C., financed by donations from local businesses. In addition to a visit to the White House, this field trip provides students with opportunities to dine in some fine restaurants, which are chosen to represent the countries and cultures studied during this particular semester.

For over two decades the experiential program has been offered to students on an optional basis. Ever since its inception, there has always been a list of applicants waiting to get admitted to the program.

THE SCHOOL ADMINISTRATION

Having been the principal of Capitol High for the past twenty-five years, Dr. Russel Wade feels a close identity with the program. His pride in the program and his perception of it as *his* program are no secrets. Last year was Dr. Wade's final year. His retirement speech focused on the American Studies program. He spoke about the success of the program and the national attention it had received in professional journals and textbooks. Dr. Wade's pride in the program was understandable: He had given it twenty years of solid support.

Last year after Dr. Wade was replaced as principal of Capitol High by Dr. Bob Gibson, several problems began to emerge. Randy Harper, a first-year social studies teacher, found himself in the middle of the worst of these problems. How or when he became so mixed up in the situation was a mystery to him. In late spring of last year when he interviewed for his current teaching position, the former principal promised him a free hand to experiment with new methods. Now, a year later, as he ponders his dilemma, Randy remembers his first few months at Capitol High. He was a graduate of the local university's department of secondary education, had taken an experiential secondary sophomore block (a six-credit-hour course taught by Dr. Higgins), and had been placed in the American Studies program for his prestudent teaching field-experience assignment. Thus, Randy was familiar with the program and was elated to have an opportunity to become a permanent Capitol High American Studies faculty member.

During those first weeks, Dr. Gibson attended a few of Randy's classes. Randy felt good about the visits because he interpreted them as evidence of Dr. Gibson's interest in the program. Soon it became obvious that Dr. Gibson's reasons for visiting the program were to evaluate the program's effectiveness.

THE INCIDENT

Last Monday Dr. Gibson was visiting when Randy introduced a new six-week unit titled "The History of the American Studies Program." Randy began the instruction by telling the students that this unit would be totally experientially based. Students were to form investigation committees and interview people in the school and in the community to develop a history of the program. Some unique aspects of this unit would be no reading assignments, no homework, and no written evaluations. Students would use tape recorders to gather the information. They would then make videotapes to transmit this information to Randy and to their classmates. The videotape presentations would be discussed by the entire class. Randy explained that this was an experimental approach. If it proved successful, he might pattern the rest of the year's units on this approach.

The next morning, Randy was summoned to Dr. Gibson's office, where he was chastised for his unorthodox approach. First, Dr. Gibson explained, the other students will question the inequality of excusing entire classes of students from all homework assignments for an entire six-week period. Second, Dr. Gibson thought the idea very poor because he is held accountable for the number of students who do poorly on the state competency exams. Third, the parents would question the absence of written assignments and homework, and especially the absence of written exams. In any case, the school district suggests nightly homework assignments and requires a minimum of two exams each six-week period.

Dr. Gibson explained, "You social studies teachers, of all people, should know that this country has become a major force because of competition. By basing grades on group projects and by replacing objective exams with presentations, you remove the competition and thereby destroy the students' motivation to succeed."

In a few short minutes, Randy's enthusiasm for both his new profession and his special assignment had been destroyed. Now he felt insecure and angry. How could a principal be so critical? He had heard Randy introduce the unit as an experimental approach. If teachers aren't allowed to experiment with new approaches, how can they improve? Randy was stunned.

THE CHALLENGE: You are Randy Harper. How will you respond?

KEY ISSUES FOR STUDY:

1. This is Dr. Gibson's first year at Capitol High. How might this affect his attitude toward the American Studies program?
2. This is Randy Harper's first year of teaching. How should this affect his reaction to Dr. Gibson's reprimand?
3. The American Studies program has over two decades of successful operation. Should this alone earn Randy the benefit of the doubt?
4. Randy's unit reflects the experiential "hands on" quality that is basic to the American Studies program, and experiential education is a nationally acclaimed approach to teaching. Should this earn any credibility for this program?
5. The previous principal, Dr. Russel Wade, had perceived the American Studies program as his "pride and joy." What does this indicate relative to a teacher's need to understand the current principal's philosophy?
6. Through his secondary methods courses and prestudent teaching field assignment, Randy has had previous experience with the American Studies program. He has chosen to develop further his expertise in experiential education by teaching in such a program. How far should a teacher go to defend teaching strategies?

7. During his previous visits to Randy's classes, Dr. Gibson gave no indication of his displeasure with Randy's teaching. Should Randy remind Dr. Gibson of this fact?

8. Can you think of ways to earn the administration's support of new programs and new teaching strategies?

SUGGESTED READINGS

Blase, J. J., & Wells, G. R. (1987). Teacher survival techniques and the most inept principals. *American Secondary Education*, *15*(4), 21–24.

Ingram, Jane, Henson, K. T., & Crew, Adolph. (1984). American studies at central high. *Phi Delta Kappan*, *66*, 296–297.

Levine, D. V. (1985). Change and innovation in the secondary curriculum. *Education Digest*, *51*, 21–23.

La Counte, M. F. (1986). Middle school for mudville? A simulation in the politics of change. *Middle School Journal*, *17*, 20–21.

Ohanian, S. (1986). What I didn't need was an interfering principal. *Learning*, *14*, 44–45.

Pink, W. T. (1986). Facilitating change at the school level: A missing factor in school reform. *Urban Review*, *18*(1), 19–30.